God's Eclipse

God Has Not
Always Been Silent

Other Works by the Author

Discovering the Mystery
of the Unity of God

The Tri-unity of God is Jewish

God in Eclipse

*God Has Not
Always Been Silent*

by John B. Metzger

God in Eclipse: God Has Not Always Been Silent
© 2013
John B. Metzger, author
www.PromisesToIsrael.org
Published by JHousePublishing under the Purple Raiment
    label, "Love Letters," Keller, TX

ISBN: 978-0-9765252-6-4
Second printing (1,500 copies)

Library of Congress Control Number: 2013933082

REL006210   RELIGION / Biblical Studies / Old Testament
REL006090   RELIGION / Biblical Criticism &
             Interpretation / Old Testament
PHI022000   PHILOSOPHY / Religious

Scripture in this book has been quoted from the following Bible versions. If not noted otherwise, Harkavy was used.

Harkavy, Alexander. *The Holy Scriptures*. New York: Hebrew Publishing Co, 1936.

Berlin, Adele, and Marc Zvi Brettler. *The Jewish Study Bible* [JSB]. New York: Oxford University, 2004.

Scofield, C. I. *The Scofield Study Bible: The Holy Bible* [KJV]. New York, NY: Oxford University Press, 1996.

Cover design: Jesse Gonzales
Editor: Joni Prinjinski
Paperback: Acid-free paper
Printed in the USA

Purple Raiment
Love Letters

Dedicated to

J. Albert Ford

As a youth I was tired of church because I found it boring and hypocritical. At my request, my parents changed churches, and I met a pastor that excited me in the Scriptures. That was back in the early 1960s. It was Pastor J. Albert Ford, the first pastor of McLean Bible Church in McLean, VA. I am writing this out of respect and love for his teaching and to honor this faithful servant. It was Pastor Ford who first instilled in me the love of the Scriptures as he opened up the Word of Life and taught me that the Bible was indeed relevant and applicable for today. In tandem with that, he taught and instilled in me a love for Israel. As I came to understand the Scriptures through his skillful teaching, he, as an instrument in the hands of G-d, placed in my heart a love for Israel and showed me the heart of G-d for His Chosen People. The foundation that he laid prepared my heart years later for the teachings of Arnold Fruchtenbaum and the writing of this book.

Table of Contents

ix

Chapter One:
God in Eclipse

Introduction

The subject of the nature of G-d is a very difficult and complex issue for us as humans to understand. So how can we know G-d in all His complexity? Is it by being Jewish? Is it by living a pious lifestyle? Is it by being obedient to the teachings of the rabbis? Is it by acts of repentance, good deeds and charity?

How can we know the person of G-d? The answer is not outside the Old Testament [Hebrew Scriptures] such as in eastern religions or manmade philosophy. It is in the Hebrew Scriptures that man can find a personal relationship with the G-d of Abraham, Isaac and Jacob. If you are a Jewish man or woman reading this book, this is the G-d of your fathers. You may be searching spiritually for meaning to life, and after all G-d is a person who is Spirit. Yet I have heard so many of my Jewish friends say that G-d was distant and out of reach. Why does He seem so mysterious, even aloof?

Let me introduce myself to you because I really want to interact with you. I am a Gentile Christian minister, born in New Jersey and have spent almost all my life in the Northeast, particularly in Pennsylvania and New York as well as the Washington D.C. area. I have many Jewish friends, and I am committed to the State of Israel and to the Jewish people, and that has been the case from my youth.

Let me assure you from the beginning that I am not a Christian trying to be Jewish. In the pursuit of meaning in my faith, I have discovered the roots of the Christian faith from the Hebrew Scriptures. I have found the *Tanakh*[1] to be rich, meaningful and exciting as I immerse myself in it and learn about the nature, and essence of G-d. I am personally inspired as I read from Moses, the Prophets and the Psalms the plan that the G-d of Abraham, Isaac and Jacob has laid out in His Word. The words of the prophets now just jump off the pages at me as I see how the teachings of the Prophets and the messages of the Psalms interact with the themes that originated with Moses. I also see how many of the words of Moses and the prophets have been fulfilled in the person of Jesus Christ [*Yeshua Mashiach*[2]] in the New Testament. I understand better the future fulfillment of the Abrahamic, Land, Davidic and New Covenants in the *Tanakh* and how they will be ultimately fulfilled in *Yeshua*. I would like to share some of my discoveries with you in the hope that you too will find the *L-RD* as an intimate person who wants to fellowship with you, of the nation He has called His people.

In my interaction with you I want to ask you what the title of this book might mean to you. Who or what is eclipsing your relationship with the L-RD? From Judaism's perspective, G-d has been silent since the prophet Malachi in the Hebrew Scriptures. That gap has lasted some 2400 years. What do you make of that? G-d has not spoken through the rabbis during this time, for none of them has ever spoken in the Name of the L-RD as Moses and the Prophets did, so

---

[1] The Hebrew term *Tanakh* is an acronym derived from the Hebrew words *Torah, Nevi'im, Kethuvim*, or the Law, the Prophets and the Writings (poetry and wisdom literature).
[2] Jesus Christ in Hebrew is *Yeshua ha Mashiach*.

why the silence? The question often comes to the conscious mind because of history: Where was G-d when we needed him? Did G-d really die in the Holocaust? Enough has happened to cause many Jewish men and women to doubt G-d's goodness or even His existence.

In Search of Intelligent Answers

We know, and it is practical to believe, that G-d created the heavens and the earth; it is not reasonable, nor scholarly, nor is it even logical to simply accept evolutionary process as an explanation for all the intricacy of life, as if order could come by random chance. Our planet and the universe that surrounds us is simply too complex to sweep G-d under the rug so to speak. Our eyes are so intricately designed that even Darwin had to admit that there must be a designer behind it all.[3] Just look at the photographs that Hubble has sent back to us from space. They are simply awesome! Look at the complexity and intricacy of life whether it be the plant or animal kingdom. Human life is so complex that we should be marveling at His craftsmanship because it is so well organized, synchronized and planned out. Being an atheist simply is not logical. Yet the question remains: *Can we know Him, our Creator? Why has He distanced Himself from us? Where is He? Does He care?*

To add to the confusion, so-called religious people have done horrible things in the Name of G-d. Notably, down through the centuries, christendom[4] has committed many

---

[3] Darwin, Charles. *The Origin of Species*, (London: J.M. Dent & Sons Ltd, 1971.), p. 167.

[4] Because of the disgraceful conduct of the Christian church towards Jewish people I have chosen in this book not to capitalize the words christian, christianity or christendom when referring to

3

atrocities against your fathers in the name of "that man"[5] from Nazareth, culminating in the Holocaust of WWII. Where was G-d? While creation itself seems reasonable to proceed from G-d and show His presence and order, anti-Semitic behavior is erratic and evil. Do Moses and the Prophets give an answer?

Again we may ask the question as to why G-d seems eclipsed from our understanding. Not only has the G-d of your fathers seemed to distance Himself from His people, but the historic christian church has been more than a thorn in your side. History has shown and many of your fathers and grandfathers have born witness to the fact that the organized christian church has turned out to be the most anti-Semitic organization on the planet. See Appendix 4 for more information on this unfortunate history.[6]

---

their apostate actions. When it is capitalized these words are referencing the true New Testament Faith.

[5] That Man: This is a phrase used by Jewish people over the years to even avoid using the name of Jesus [*Yeshua*].

[6] Appendix 4 provides excellent, well-written resources for those who are not yet aware of the long history of persecution of the Jewish people by the traditional, organized church. Most Jewish people are well aware of what their parents, grandparents and other ancestors suffered at the hands of so-called Christians, so this need not be belabored in this book. Because anti-Semitism is on the rise worldwide, most Jewish men, women, and children living today have had their own personal encounters with anti-Semitism as well. Olivier Melnick's recent book, *They Have Conspired Against You: Responding to the New Anti-Semitism*, provides timely, positive suggestions for all honest people with good intentions, to help them recognize and guard against the ravages of anti-Semitism. While many are not aware of it, our precious freedoms are being attacked by the same new torrent of destructive anti-Semitism being unleashed.

If we can manage to sidestep the history of enmity and contention, it is possible to make a reasonable assessment of the *legitimate* differences between Judaism and New Testament Faith. These differences can be seen to revolve around perceptions of G-d's nature itself. Is He one or three-in-one? Is He a G-d of love, or one of hatred? Does He change His mind, or is He consistent? However one may answer such questions, the ramifications of ignorance as to the difference between these two belief systems led to the christian atrocities from the 4th century CE onward to the present day. There is no logical explanation that can defend the pogroms, crusades, inquisition and Holocaust nor the political persecution that exists today as a result of christian ignorance or hatred, either on an individual or organized level.

G-d does not take anti-Semitism lightly (Genesis 12:3); judgment will come to those who are anti-Semitic or to be more precise anti-Jewish.[7] Christianity has its authoritative source, the New Testament, alongside the Hebrew Scriptures, to tell true Christians how to live before their fellow men, the Jewish people, and how to conduct themselves before a holy G-d.

In this work, I wish to put into simple language a debunking of the issues surrounding G-d's nature. This clarity can defeat the type of hatred and confusion that

---

[7] *Anti-Semitism* means literally being against those who speak Semitic languages (e.g. Arabs, Ethiopians, or Assyrians). In practice, however, it refers to the persecution only of Jewish people, either as individuals or a group, or even as a State, such as being against the modern State of Israel. The term does not apply to Arabs or other Semitic people, just to Jewish people. So the term anti-Semitic needs to be understood as being against the Jewish people, anti-Jewish.

comes from ignorance of what the G-d of Abraham, Isaac and Jacob has said in His Word. With clarity comes clear thinking, and the ability to intelligently consider who G-d is, and how we might relate to Him.

Does anti-Semitism come from the Christian New Testament? While it is true that the theological issue of G-d becoming a man has been rejected by most Jewish people, christendom most cruelly took that rejection and used it as a club against the Jewish people. Such conduct cannot be excused, but that does not mean that the New Testament was wrong in its teaching, just twisted by corrupted theology and wrongly used by corrupted people. However, to be cautious, I will rely on the teachings of the *Tanakh* in the examination of the question at hand of how a man or woman on a spiritual journey might seek the face of a G-d in eclipse.

There are two principal triggers that lay at the core of christian anti-Semitism:

1. There are two completing belief systems on the nature of G-d:
   - Is He an absolute "one" according to Judaism, or
   - Is He a "plurality in one" as New Testament faith says?

2. The second area of contention is not legitimate because of the false doctrine taken on by christendom coupled with their complete arrogance, pride, and smug self-righteousness as they acted against your fathers. Accusing them, and perhaps you, of killing Jesus or "killing G-d" and all the pogroms, the crusades, the inquisition and the Holocaust that resulted is only the tip of the iceberg because of the

different responses in understanding the nature of G-d.

By the very words recorded in the New Testament, christendom stands guilty and condemned before the G-d of Israel. By that same source of authority—the New Testament—in G-d's court of law, christendom and its dealing with your fathers stand condemned before His holiness, righteousness, and justice and will be judged by Him for it.

Most of my Jewish friends have told me they had given up on G-d on several fronts: given up on religious piety or given up on the religious zeal of the rabbis and their teachings. Some, regardless of the branch of Judaism they follow, have repackaged their religious faith to make it more palatable for the 21st century. Others within the religious community find all the rabbinic studies empty, but continue in the charade personally because of family, business and social pressures, as they do not want to be ostracized.

The rabbis do not have the answer to the question: *How can we know G-d and have a personal relationship and communion with Him?* Yet many ponder this question and others that are directly related to it. Let me offer four clusters of questions that you at some time in your life may have pondered:

1. Where did we come from? Who made me as a person and chose Israel as a nation and why?

2. Who are we? What is our value and purpose on this earth?

3. What has gone wrong with the world? Why do evil, suffering, war, death, decay and injustice exist?

4. Can we do anything to fix the disconnects and evil? Is man the cause of these problems? Does man have the solutions?

These are disturbing questions to anyone with spiritual sensitivity. Do philosophy and science have the answers to life? Does man in all his intelligence have the answers to life?

What about common sense? Can we gain a practical sense of meaning in our lives by centering on the goodness of mankind? Tragically many Jewish people will believe in the goodness of man rather than understanding the depravity of man, as illustrated by Anne Frank who did not survive the Holocaust. She stated in her diary:

> It's really a wonder that I haven't dropped all my ideals … Yet I keep them, because in spite of everything I still believe that people are really good at heart.[8]

Being Jewish and knowing all that you have and are suffering at the hands of anti-Jewish Hamans, it should be self-evident that trusting in the goodness of man and trying to be the master of one's fate by pulling oneself up by the bootstraps of meritorious self-goodness is self-limiting. Even the good-hearted belief that man can make the world a better place seems intuitively disproven by experience. Why does man still experience the same evils of the ages? Why are Jewish people still hated instead of being admired for their place in history and in light of all of their individual and collective contributions in medicine, physics and science that benefit so many? Why is their historical preservation of

---

[8] Copied from a plague at the entrance for the Saint Petersburg, Florida, Holocaust Museum.

the *Tanakh* not recognized with the respect deserved for the contribution it has made to civilization in general?

After millenniums of human existence it becomes quite evident that man is not in the driver's seat of his life. Is G-d, who is also called the *L-RD* or *HaShem*[9] [the Name], still sitting on His throne in heaven? Can He reveal to us the meaning and purpose in life?

Is the *Tanakh* silent on all these matters that escape our management? Has G-d forgotten His promises to the Jewish people? Or could it be that the G-d of your fathers has all the answers needed to comfort and satisfy the Jewish heart woven throughout the Hebrew Scriptures for those who desire to behold them?

---

[9] "The Name," Hebrew alternative for the divine Name, *L-RD* [*YHVH*].

Chapter Two:
G-d's First-Born

A Mystery the Rabbis Cannot Explain

Examples of the attachment of G-d the Father to Israel His first-born son abound in Scripture. What intense joy! What identification and nurture pour out in a flood of love bestowed on a first-born. To G-d the Father the nation of Israel is His first-born.[10] The law of Moses speaks of the blessings and duties of the first-born son. The relationship is unique.

What has happened to cause a separation between *HaShem* and His first-born son, Israel? The prophet Hosea said something very interesting as he spoke prophetically to Israel in Hosea 5:15-6:1:

> *And I will return to My abode – Till they realize their guilt. In their distress, they will seek me and beg for My favor. Come, let us turn back to the LORD: He attacked, and He can heal us; He wounded, and He can bind us up.*

What does G-d mean by returning to His abode until Israel realizes their guilt? When did He leave His abode that He would have to return to it? What is Israel's guilt or offense

---

[10] Exodus 4:2

that they must repent of? He also says that Israel will return to Him in the future.

The inferences of this should capture your attention because today the footsteps of Messiah are near. The end times, the *Time of Jacob's trouble*,[11] also known as the last days, are the days that immediately precede the coming of the Messiah to set up the promised Kingdom.

In reading the prophets Jeremiah and Hosea, you will find that *HaShem* "divorced" ancient Judah (Jeremiah 3:18) and Israel (Hosea 2:2) because of their sins against Him. These divorces correlate to the two major captivities that removed the Jewish people from the Land of Israel. No "remarriage" between Israel and the G-d of Israel was recorded in the Hebrew Scriptures. Yet Moses, Isaiah, Jeremiah, Hosea, and Zechariah all speak of Israel in the future once again being G-d's people and that all Israel will worship Him alone (Jeremiah 31:31-34; Ezekiel 36:26-28). Moses spoke words to Israel that refer to a sin that Israel did and the hardships that Israel would suffer in Leviticus 26:40-41:

If they shall confess their iniquity and the iniquity of their fathers, in that they trespassed against Me, yea, were hostile to Me. When I, in turn have been hostile to them and have removed them into the land of their enemies, then at last shall their uncircumcised heart humble itself, and they atone for their iniquity.

What was the trespass that caused G-d to place your fathers in the lands of the Gentiles? What is the trespass that was committed that must be dealt with before the L-RD

---

[11] Jeremiah 30:7

remembers His covenant with Abraham, Isaac and Jacob? What does He mean by the *uncircumcised heart*? These are probing questions. Do you know the answers? Do your rabbis know the answers?

Rabbis, why have the Jewish people of Israel left Judaism in droves? Eighty percent of the Jewish people in the Land have abandoned religious Judaism. Why? Evidently among rabbis the answer is not known. The *Tanakh* gives the answer: Are you interested to see what *HaShem* said and to respond to Him?

A New Mystery for Today

What could it mean that the State of Israel has been restored after over 2400 years of dispersion to Gentile lands? Is this prophetic? Yes, according to Ezekiel 37. G-d is moving Jewish people to return to the Land so that He can purify Israel. Once again there will be in the future a remarriage between G-d and Israel when Israel will have a *circumcised heart* (Deuteronomy 30:6)? How is a physical return to the Land related to the heart issues in the inner being of a person? What is the trespass that Moses references in Leviticus 26:40-41 that would prevent the spiritual reunion of the people in the Land with their G-d? What is the offense towards *HaShem* according to the prophet Hosea (5:15-6:3) that still needs healing? If such spiritual questions do tug at your heart, or if you are intellectually curious as to what the Scriptures may say of relevance to Jewish people today, then this book is written for you.

True believers are NOT one and the same with corrupted christendom. It is my sole intension to concentrate on what the *Tanakh* presents concerning the person of G-d and how He revealed Himself to your fathers, Abraham, Moses and the Prophets. Are you up to it? What you are about to read will depart from what corrupted christendom has taught regarding the Jewish people. My approach will be to look directly at the Hebrew Scriptures alone instead of relying on the rationalizations of the rabbis or other religious teachers. Are you willing to investigate your Scripture, the Hebrew Scriptures, the *Tanakh*, or let someone else think and interpret for you?

A key divide between the two historic faiths of Christianity and Judaism concerns a contrasting understanding of the very nature of G-d. I contend that the *Tanakh* itself is rich with revelation as to G-d's true nature. The Hebrew Scriptures provide a picture of G-d as a plural unity-in-one. As we investigate the many passages from the *Tanakh*, it becomes clear that the Christian concept of a "New Testament G-d" with a separate identity from the *Tanakh* is inaccurate. At the same time, the detailed revelation from the *Tanakh* regarding G-d's plural unity does not match up with the teachings of the rabbis of an absolute monotheism. If one looks clearly at the Scriptures, the teachings of the *Tanakh* and the New Testament are not contradictory, but complementary – each a revelation of the same G-d with a consistent nature.

This key understanding of G-d's nature unlocks the mystery of how Jewish people can relate to their G-d, with full confidence from the revelation of the Hebrew Scriptures. This understanding is also able to inform Gentile Christians of G-d's enduring, unchanging nature from everlasting to everlasting.

I stand amazed at the *Tanakh* and the covenant that G-d made with your father Abraham. *HaShem* also confirmed the Abrahamic Covenant to Isaac and Jacob. I have observed that you are the most unique people on earth. You excel in

14

every field of endeavor far beyond your population in respect to all other ethnicities because of the promises of that covenant, except in one area, the study of the *Tanakh* itself. I want to challenge you intellectually and spiritually to look for yourself at the words of *HaShem* as He revealed Himself to your fathers and to you. Let us see what has eclipsed the Jewish people from their G-d. Please join me as we look together at your Scriptures. I believe that intelligent answers are at hand if you will be patient.

Chapter Three:
How Do We Describe G-d in Relation to Man?

In my conversation with my Jewish friends they have said that Jewish people today have no personal relationship with G-d, the G-d of Israel for assorted reasons:

- G-d does not exist;

- The G-d of the miracles in the *Tanakh* is a myth thus He is not worth committing oneself to;

- If we are His chosen people where was He during the Holocaust?

- We do not have a temple or sacrifices so how can we relate to Him, besides sacrifices are outdated?

- Our rabbis have burdened us with so many irrelevant laws so why bother.

- We are tired of looking different with all the traditional clothing and practices;

- We are tired of looking for the Messiah as our hopes are always dashed to the ground. We will make the world a better place by ourselves; He is not a person to come but a messianic movement.

- The G-d of the *Tanakh* is not relevant to the 21st century.

These and other things have disheartened the Jewish people making them feel very distant from the G-d of their fathers Abraham, Isaac and Jacob. Some Jewish young people, after fulfilling their military commitment in the IDF, have drifted off to experiment with Hinduism and other mystical eastern religions to find the basic answers to the questions of life: Who am I? Why do I exist? What is the purpose of life? G-d cannot be intellectualized or rationalized away. So how did Abraham, Moses, Samuel, Daniel and Elijah have such a personal vibrant relationship with Him, and is it possible today? How do Jewish people comprehend G-d, His majesty, nature, character and His essence? Let us look at what G-d said about Himself and later what G-d said about man. To do so we will go to His Word given personally to you, the Jewish people. We are not interested in what religious men say about Him, whether they be a rabbi, priest or preacher. The Hebrew Scriptures were written for you to read and understand, not just for the professional religious men to lord it over you. We will start at the very beginning and pursue some very basic information about Him.

Let us begin with the Hebrew Scriptures. G-d, the sovereign of the universe has given you, the Jewish people, a book called the *Tanakh* (Hebrew Bible and called the Old Testament by Christians). As with any book, you can read things into it that the author never intended, which religious men have done whether they are rabbi, priest or preacher. So how do we prevent this in our study of the *Tanakh*? First, we have to understand that G-d as the Creator of all things in the heavens and the earth is capable of communicating to man through language, for He is also the Creator of language and grammar. G-d is the greatest communicator and He is completely capable in using language to communicate with His people for He Himself is a person. Man erroneously thinks that G-d cannot communicate very well so he tries to help out G-d by adding to Scripture their own personal interpretation. But in reality, as all religious men have done this, they confuse, misquote, deny and change what G-d said by using his own rationale in his interpretation instead of interpreting it exactly as G-d said it. Following is a good definition for interpreting the *Tanakh* as we read and study about G-d, His Word to us:

> When the plain sense of Scripture makes common sense seek no other sense; therefore, take every word at its primary, ordinary, usual, literal meaning unless the facts of the immediate context, studied in the light of related passages and axiomatic and fundamental truths, indicate clearly otherwise.[12]

This we need to ponder and refer back to often because what I have discovered for myself is that the *Talmud* and rabbinic commentaries have taken unprecedented liberties by adding information sometimes using a great degree of creative imagination to interpret and link passages that have absolutely nothing to do with the context. They make it authoritative by their religious position, thus ignoring the obvious interpretation of many passages, and christians are guilty of the same thing.

One other important issue is realizing that the *Tanakh* is *HaShem*'s Word; it is His communication to you, the Jewish people. The rabbis of the past have meticulously preserved the Scripture, protecting every word and letter as it was hand copied. So what has been handed down to you is a preserved copy of G-d's letter to you, the whole nation of Israel. Whether it is the *Torah* (Books of Moses), Prophets or Writings, the three-fold division of the *Tanakh*, it is all equally G-d's Word. We do understand that the *Torah* is foundational, but that does not make the Prophets and the Writing sections of the *Tanakh* any less the Word of G-d

---

[12] David L. Cooper, *The God of Israel* (Los Angeles, CA: Biblical Research Society, 1945), Foreword.

because *HaShem* is the author of all of it. The G-d of Abraham, Isaac and Jacob that spoke to Moses on Mt. Sinai is the same G-d that spoke through David the Psalmist, and prophets like Daniel, Isaiah, Jeremiah, Ezekiel, Hosea and Zechariah.

G-d

G-d has referred to Himself in the *Tanakh* by using the following Names: *Elohim*[13] (G-d), *El* (G-d), *Eloah* (G-d), *Elah* (G-d), *L-RD* (YHVH) and *L-rd* (*Adhonai*). Here is a brief description of the usage of these words for the G-d of Israel:

Hebrew	Name	Plural or Singular	Occurs in *Tanakh*
אלהים	*Elokim*	Plural noun	2600 times[14]
אל	*El*	Singular noun	238 times
אלוֹהַ	*Eloah*	Singular noun	57 times
אֱלָהּ	*Elah*	Singular noun	87 times
יְהֹוָה	*L-RD*: Personal Name for G-d – *YHVH*	Singular	6,828 times
אדני	*Adhonai*: Lord/Master	Plural when referring to G-d	449 times[15]

---

[13] Hereafter *Elohim* will be written as *Elokim*.

[14] Christianity spells the plural word for G-d when written in English as *Elohim*. However, orthodox and ultra-orthodox spell it *Elokim*.

[15] *Adhonai* is used in combination with *Yahweh/L-RD* 315 times, and it is now generally accepted that in Old Testament literature *adhonai* was an independent name for G-d like *elohim*, meaning "the Lord." Source: William B. Eerdmans Publishing Company's *Theological Dictionary of the Old Testament*, various editions.

Let us begin by quoting Genesis [*Bereshit*] 1:1

> *In the beginning* **God created** *the heaven and the earth.*

We want to look at the two words in bold. The word translated G-d is *Elokim* which is a plural word. How can that be because Judaism teaches that G-d is one and that is correct? But the rabbis also teach that G-d is an absolute one (one alone, standing by itself: *yachid*) and not a plural one (plurality in unity: *echad*).

Two Points

There are two points in understanding the relationship of these two words. **Point one:** if G-d is an absolute one (*yachid*) as the rabbis say, then why did Moses use a plural word for G-d to show his oneness (*echad*)? Even the psalmist in Psalm 45:6-7 [7-8][16] states that there are two *Elokim*s:

> *[6] Thy throne,* **which is of** *God* [*Elokim*], **shall stand** *forever and ever: the sceptre of thy kingdom is a right sceptre.* *[7] Thou lovest righteousness, and hatest wickedness: therefore* **God** [*Elokim*], *thy* **God** [*Elokim*], *hath anointed thee with the oil of gladness above thy fellows.*

In this passage there are two *Elokim*s, but on top of that, one *Elokim* is anointed by the other *Elokim*. Now rabbis try to

---

[16] The citations in brackets reflect the reference numbers in the Jewish Bible when they differ from the numbers for the same material presented in the Christian Bible. The Christian Bible contains all 39 books of the *Tanakh* plus the 27 books of the New Testament, but some of the Old Testament is numbered slightly differently in the Christian versions.

explain that away, but remember our method of interpretation previously quoted (see footnote 12). Note the **bolded** words in the verse from the Harkavy Translation, the words "which is of" and "shall stand" are not in the Hebrew text but added to obscure the literal meaning of the text. *Elokim* is used 2600 times in the *Tanakh*, 2350 times of the G-d of Israel, and 250 times in relation to pagan gods. An example of that is found in Exodus 20:2-3:

> *² I am the LORD thy* **God** *[Elokim], who have brought thee out of the land of Egypt, out of the house of bondage. ³ Thou shalt have no other* **gods** *[elohim] before me.*

The question that begs to be asked is: Why did Moses use *Elokim* (plural) to speak of G-d when he had two other words which were available in Hebrew, *El* and *Eloah*, which are both singular? Those singular words for G-d would better reflect the nature and essence of G-d as an absolute one [*yachid*] as the rabbis interpret it and completely eliminate any possibility of the plurality of G-d. Did G-d through Moses miscommunicate in the very first sentence of His Word His very own nature and essence to Israel thus making the *Tanakh* erroneous from the very beginning? If G-d is one as the rabbis say, why didn't G-d through Moses and the prophets use the singular words for G-d such as *El*, *Eloah*, and after the exile *Elah*, exclusively throughout the *Tanakh*? It would have effectively eliminated any future reference to the G-d of Israel being a plural unity of one [*echad*]. In Genesis 1:1 G-d is presenting his oneness, but He is also making another point.

The **second point** is that G-d through Moses is breaking grammar because the word *Elokim* is a plural noun and thus grammatically requires a plural verb to reflect the noun in case and number. However, in Genesis 1:1 that is not what G-d did. He used the noun *Elokim,* which is a plural noun, and the word *created*, which is a singular verb that does not reflect the same in case and number grammatically of the noun G-d. So why in the very first sentence of the *Tanakh* is G-d purposely breaking grammar? The plural noun *Elokim* [G-d] and the singular verb *created* simply do not match grammatically. So as G-d communicated to Moses, did G-d misquote Himself or somehow make a mistake? Or is G-d breaking grammar to make a statement for the express purpose of attracting our attention? By using a plural noun and the singular verb He is making the statement that, yes, He is one (*echad*) G-d by using the singular verb *created*. He is also stating that He is a plural unity of one (*echad*) in His use of the plural noun *Elokim*.

Why is this such a sensitive issue for Judaism? Let me answer this as follows: In the *Tanakh*, Moses prophesied in Deuteronomy 29:25 to 30:17-20 and the Prophets recorded that your fathers would choose to disobey *HaShem* and choose to worship the pagan gods. This disobedience would come after *HaShem* submitted to them the Mosaic Covenant (Exodus 24:3-8) and they committed themselves to worshipping Him alone. Because *Elokim* made a covenant with your fathers, and they committed themselves to it, *HaShem* led them out of Egypt and gave them the land that He promised Abraham, Isaac and Jacob in the Abrahamic Covenant (Genesis 12:1-3; 13:14-18; 15:1-21; 17:1-21; 22:15-18). He also said in the Land Covenant that if your fathers obeyed Him (Deuteronomy 28:1-14), He would bless them so much that they could not contain it all. However, if they disobeyed Him He would punish and judge them with the cursing in Deuteronomy 28:15-68. If disobedience continued He would send your fathers into captivity, which He did in the Assyrian and Babylonian captivities respectively. Then followed the Great Diaspora at the hands of the Romans in 70 and 135 CE, and that is history (Deuteronomy 29:1-29). G-d promised Abraham, because of his faith in *HaShem*, that he and his descendants, that is the Jewish people, would possess the Land. Why has that been so elusive and difficult? What has happened over the last 1900 years that the Jewish people have not been able to possess the Land and live in peace? The principle that *HaShem* has laid down is that the Jewish people have the title deed to the Land and nothing will break that, but the enjoyment of the Land is based on Israel's faithfulness and obedience to *HaShem* and not to religious men. Both individuals and religious leaders are accountable to Him, and that includes the rabbis too. You, as an individual or collectively as a nation, are accountable to *HaShem* for everything He has written in His Word, the *Tanakh*. However, the rabbis are even more accountable to *HaShem* as leaders if they have not reflected in their teaching what *HaShem* expects of you individually or of Israel collectively.

The religious leaders and the people after the Babylonian captivity never again wanted to be accused of idolatry and suffer through another exile. So they became very focused on the oneness (*yachid*) of *Elokim* (*HaShem*), which is understandable and spiritually responsible. However, they saw many passages referencing the plurality of *HaShem*, but they did not know what to do with those passages because they now began to focus on *HaShem* as an absolute one (*yachid*). Instead of recognizing how *HaShem* revealed Himself to Israel, they chose to rationalize away the passages that showed the plural aspect of the oneness (*echad*) of *Elokim* (*HaShem*). The Apostles of the New Testament taught that Jesus (*Yeshua*) was the fulfillment of the prophecies of Moses and the Prophets when Messiah, Son of David came in the flesh (Isaiah 9:6-7 [5-6]). But because of their exclusive focus on the absolute oneness (*yachid*) of G-d the Sanhedrin, the religious leaders of that day, led the people to reject *Yeshua* as the Messiah of Israel 40 years before the destruction of Jerusalem and the Temple, *the city and the sanctuary* (Daniel 9:26). The *Talmud*, the teaching and comments of the rabbis on the *Tanakh*, provides a couple of interesting statements. The following statement from the *Talmud* shows a gap in the rabbis' observations of history. The Babylonian Talmud states:

> Our rabbis taught: During the last forty years before the destruction of the Temple the lot ['for the Lord'] did not come up in the right hand; nor did the crimson colored strap become white; nor did the western most light shine; and the doors of the Hekel [Temple] would open by themselves (Soncino version, *Yoma* 39b).

The rabbis have never connected together the events referenced in the *Talmud* to their rejection and death of *Yeshua* as the Messiah of Israel 40 years before the destruction of the Temple.

One additional thing: The New Testament states one thing that the *Talmud* did not, which was the veil between the Holy Place and the Holy of Holies in the Temple was rent (torn) from top to bottom (Matthew 27:51-53) at the moment of death of *Yeshua*. All of these phenomena occurred 40 years before the destruction of the *city and the sanctuary* as foretold by the prophet Daniel 600 years earlier (Daniel 9:26). It was the same year that Jesus became the Passover Lamb of G-d. *HaShem* was speaking through some unusual events to your fathers, but they missed the point.[17]

---

[17] The point was that Exodus 12:3 which states that on the 10th day of the first month (Aviv/Nisan) of their year they were to take a

Why did these things happen and the rabbis not put the timing together with the death of *Yeshua* [Jesus] *the Lamb of God* (John 1:29, 35) for the sins of all people both Jew and Gentile? *Yeshua* was the one whom Isaiah spoke of as the Suffering Servant of *HaShem* in Isaiah 52:13 to 53:12.

The Sanhedrin of the first century refused to see the connection and dug in their heels about Jesus not being the Messiah. This made a theological divide between Jewish people who rejected Jesus and those Jewish people who embraced Him. It is estimated in the first century CE that 20 to 30 percent of Jewish people in Jerusalem, Judea, and Galilee embraced Jesus as their Messiah. Now couple the Sanhedrin's rejection with the corruption of the church and all its atrocities upon Jewish people by organized christianity from the 4th century CE to today. This has served only to further reinforce the rabbis rejection of *Yeshua* as Messiah among the people.

So here we are in the 21st century, twenty centuries after the death and resurrection of Jesus, and my Jewish friends expressed as mentioned before that Judaism is not relevant and G-d is not there. Jewish people have been disappointed and disillusioned over the centuries in looking for the Messiah and the fulfillment of the promises by accepting 46

---

lamb and observe the lamb for four days to make sure it was a perfect lamb without spot or blemish. Then on the 14th day the lamb became the Passover lamb. In the Gospels of the New Testament we discover the timing when *Yeshua* entered into Jerusalem riding on the donkey (Zechariah 9:9): It was the 10th day of the first month of their year and was observed by the Pharisees, Scribes, Sadducees and the Herodians for four days, and they could find no fault in *Yeshua* and on the 14th day He became G-d's Passover Lamb just as John the Baptist had introduced Him, *Behold the Lamb of God that takes away the sin of the world* (Gospel of John 1:29).

false messiahs, with the last one being Menachem Schneerson who lived in New York City.[18] The prophet Ezekiel gives the Word of *HaShem* in chapter 37:11. Ezekiel paints a verbal picture of the feeling and heart of Jewish people and what they will say in the last days:

> *Son of man, these bones are the whole house of Israel: behold, they say, Our bones are dried up, and our hope is lost: we are clean cut off.*

Here is the heart of Jewish people today speaking through Ezekiel: *Where is G-d? Where is the Messiah? Where is the hope of the promises that our fathers have told us of?* Yet with each disappointment, each anti-Semitic act, where is G-d? Our hope is gone! Yet the testimony and words of Moses and the Prophets were not consulted. *HaShem* has not spoken to the Jewish people since the prophet Malachi 2400 years ago, yet *HaShem* has not cast you out and He has not washed His hands of the Jewish people.

Jewish people are tired of being persecuted simply because they are Jewish and as a result of the labels that the organized apostate church has placed over their heads through the centuries. The nations around Israel seek its destruction; Europe does not like the existence of Israel and in 50 years Islam will have a majority among European populations. All the other nations are playing political games with Israel, including the United States. Where does that leave the Jewish people? It leaves you without hope for the promised Kingdom, a better world that many in secular, Reform and Conservative Judaism are trying to achieve. The world is corrupting itself more than ever, and Israel is

---

[18] See the New Testament Gospel of Matthew 24:3-7.

on the outside looking in just wanting peace and freedom to live in safety. The simple desire is to raise their families without continued threats from the world and suicide bombers, murderers, rockets from the Hamas in Gaza and the Hezbollah in Lebanon plus all the hate speech and propaganda directed at Israel from the Islamic world and other anti-Semites.

So the question that you need to ask yourself biblically is why are all these things happening to the Jewish people? With centuries of being trodden underfoot by the Gentiles, why is G-d completely silent? Why? Isn't it reasonable for you to search for the answer from G-d's Word instead of being continually influenced by the writings and words of rabbinic Judaism which cannot offer a biblical answer based on the words of Moses and the Prophets? As you proceed through this book and study the plural references to *HaShem* as well as the numerous passages that deal with the deity of Messiah, make a close and personal examination of these passages and think for yourself.

In the Image and Likeness of Elokim

In the *Torah*,[19] the Books of Moses, there is a verse that in a brief and general way says how G-d created mankind, and it is found in Genesis 1:26-27:

> [26] *And God said, "**let us** make man in **our image**, after **our likeness**. They shall rule the fish of the sea, the birds of the sky, the cattle, the whole earth, and all the creeping things that creep on the earth.* [7]

[19] The term Torah is used by Judaism as a very elastic term. It is used from one teaching point to all of the Talmud and Midrash writings. However, in this book it is used only of the Five Books of Moses.

> *And God created* **man** *in His image, in the image of*
> *God He created* **him***;* **male and female** *He created*
> **them***.* [Emphasis is mine.] (Jewish Study Bible)

G-d created mankind in His image and likeness. We saw in Genesis 1:1 that the word for G-d is *Elokim* and it is a plural word. Again this is strange for if *Elokim* is an absolute one [*yachid*] then why did the great law giver Moses use the plural word *Elokim* when he had two singular words available (*El* or *Eloah*)?

When *Elokim* created on the other days of creation it says, *And G-d* [*Elokim*] *said, Let there be ... and it was so* in verses 6, 9, 11, 14, 20, and 24. It was very impersonal, generic and matter of fact statement. However, *Elokim* in verse 26 does the complete opposite by becoming very personal. On the other days of creation Moses used the word *min* meaning kind or species. With the creation of man *min* is not used, for man is the crown of G-d's creation. Man was not created by *Elokim* as a kind or species but a unique creation like Himself when He said; *Let* **us** *make man in* **our** *image and after* **our** *likeness.* We were not made (or evolved) from or like the animals, but made by *Elokim* to be like *Elokim*. Rabbis say that the plural "us" of *Elokim* refers to the angels of heaven who are in consultation with G-d in the great council of G-d. There is one huge fatal flaw with that argument: there are no angels in the context nor are the angels ever mentioned as part of the council of G-d. Remember all the wisdom that G-d wanted the angels to possess was given to them by *Elokim* Himself. So why would He need their consultation to begin with (Isaiah 40:13-14)? It is *Elokim* plural that is speaking and then acting in the singular in verse 27 *and He created them.* *Elokim* with complete dominion over all things in the heavens and the earth created man to *rule* as a subordinate to have dominion over the earth. This is meant to be a parallel. *Elokim*, plural, rules over the universe and man (male and female) plural, was to have dominion over the earth under the authority of G-d. This is a biblical picture and not a manmade system of evolution which denies the creative mind, person and intellect of *Elokim*, which places man as an evolved animal.

Elokim is the speaker in Genesis 1:26 and He makes a very unusual statement, Let *us make man*. Not only does *Elokim* reflect Himself as a plural person who made man after His image and likeness, but He uses a first person plural pronoun. Does that mean that *Elokim* has a body with arms, legs, hands and feet? Absolutely not! *Elokim* is pure spirit, so how did *Elokim* create us after His image and likeness? *Elokim* is a person and He created mankind as people, persons like Himself although limited. He has emotion (feeling, love, grief, and patience), intellect (mind) and will (the ability to decide). He can make a plan and schedule it with intricate detail. He can look at creation and say *it is good*. We also have emotion, intellect and will and we too can look at the product of our minds and hands that we have made with great satisfaction and accomplishment. We are persons, unique personalities above all of creation. Many things have been said over the years about how man is like *Elokim*, but one point is distinctly clear. According to His Word He references Himself as plural when He created the heavens and the earth. He also references Himself in the plural when He created mankind in the plural.

Elokim made mankind as a person, in His image and likeness, He made us, mankind (Hebrew word is *adam*) male and female, plural, in His image for He is plural according to the meaning of *Elokim*. He rules the universe as *Elokim* as we as mankind are to rule or have dominion over the earth in the plural, male and female. What becomes interesting is that *Elokim*, plural, when He created, created in the singular according to Genesis 1:27 because everything that *Elokim* does, He does as *one* (*echad*).

Elokim created us in His image and likeness when He created male and female or mankind in the plural. We reflect Him as a person, so we are plural.

A second aspect is very interesting. Each individual person is made in the plural. To be exact, we are three in one. Each of us has a body, soul and spirit, yet we are one (*echad*). When you look at another human being you only see his body, you do not see his soul and spirit which are invisible. The *Tanakh* presents *HaShem Elokim*, the same way. It presents three who are one as we are three in one, made in His image and likeness. *HaShem Elokim* became visible to Abraham, Moses, Joshua, Gideon as well as others in the form of the Angel or Messenger of *HaShem*, while the other two persons of *Elokim* remain invisible. Bare all this in mind as we look at *Elokim* through the Law, Prophets and the Writings.

This may be foreign to you, but challenge the status quo, question and read with your heart (Deuteronomy 6:5; 10:12; 11:13) the Hebrew Scriptures, for the *Tanakh* is *Elokim*'s book to you. You do not need to read and study under rabbis using rabbinic commentaries that you have largely rejected because they have been part of the problem. I would like to quote from some rabbinic sources to show just how rabbinic Judaism in their attempts to be faithful have actually undermined the authority of *HaShem*'s Word and placed their words (Oral Law) as the ones to be revered more than *HaShem*'s. Look at these statements and then ask what has eclipsed your G-d from you:

It is more punishable to act against the words of the scribe then those of the Scriptures.

He that says something that he did not hear from his rabbi causes the *shekinah* to depart from Israel.

He that would contradict his rabbi is as he that would contradict the shekinah. He that would speak against his rabbi is as he that would speak against G-d.

My son give more heed to the words of the rabbi than to the words of the Mosaic Law.

Our rabbi's taught to be engaged in the study of scripture is neither good or bad. But to be engaged in the study of the Mishnah [rabbinic interpretation] is a good habit and brings reward. But, as to the laws of the Scribes, whoever transgresses any of the enactments of the Scribes incurs the penalty of death. Tractate *Eruvin* 21b.

He who occupies himself with Scripture gains what is no merit. He who occupies himself with Mishnah gains merit for the people receive a reward. He who occupies himself with Talmud—there is no source of greater merit than this. *Talmud*, *Shabbat* 15c and *Baba Metzia* 33a.

Some teachings were handed on orally, and some things were handed on in writing … we conclude that the ones handed on orally are more precious. *Hagigah* 1:7b

> Anyone who disregards the Mishnah, and does not act in accordance with its teachings, 'has despised the word of the *LORD*. *Sanhedrin* 99a

Notice these eight rabbinic statements come from the *Talmud* and each one diminishes the authority of the Scriptures.[20] Is it possible that rabbinic Judaism is the object that has caused the eclipse between Israel and their G-d?

Elokim wrote the Scriptures to you, for you, to show you His love and compassion for you, for great is *HaShem's* love for Israel (Deuteronomy 7:7-8; Zephaniah 3:17; Zechariah 2:12). But rabbinic Judaism has superseded *HaShem's* Word with their own.

It is not just rabbinic Judaism that has done intellectual reinterpretation of the *Tanakh*. Some christians have done the same thing with their New Testament by spiritualizing the text beyond recognition to fulfill a preconceived bias.

Who is the L-RD or HaShem?

Now let us look at the very Name of *HaShem*, יְהֹוָה, which is not pronounced or written by the Orthodox—first because the pronunciation has been lost, and secondly for fear of profaning or blaspheming His Name in using it wrongly. It is an educated guess as to the pronunciation of G-d's Name, but it is written and spoken in the *Tanakh* as *L-RD*, *Yahweh* or *Jehovah*. *Elokim* gave this Name, יְהֹוָה, to the Israelites through Moses as His personal covenant Name for them to call Him.

---

[20] in tractates *Berachot* 3:2; *Sanhedrin* 11:3; 99a; *Yevamot* 89b-90a; *Eruvin* 21b

L-RD is used in the *Tanakh* 6,828 times, and as stated earlier in this chapter it is a singular name for *Elokim* and is used that way all the time. Yet even with this singular, personal word for the covenant-keeping G-d of Israel there are plural references. Let me briefly give you three passages:

> *The LORD rained upon Sodom and Gomorrah*
> *sulfurous fire from the LORD out of heaven*
> (Genesis 19:24.)

There is much that can be said about this passage as you go back to Genesis 18, but it will suffice to say there are two *L-RDs* referenced in this passage. So not only does *Elokim*, a plural word, show plurality, but the singular word *L-RD* can be used by *Elokim* to show plurality. In the Prophets there are two more references that show the same thing. In Hosea 1:2-7 the *L-RD* is speaking in verses 2, 4, and 6, and in verse 7 He states He will deliver Israel by sending another *L-RD* who is Israel's *Elokim*:

> *But I [L-RD] will have mercy upon the house of*
> *Judah, and will save them by the LORD their God*
> *[Elokim].*

Here not only are there two *L-RDs*, but the second *L-RD* is identified as their *Elokim* being sent by the first *L-RD* to save them (Judah). Isaiah 44:6 and 54:5 also points to two *L-RDs*:

> *Thus saith the LORD the king of Israel, and his*
> *redeemer the LORD of hosts; I am the first, and I am*
> *the last; and besides me there is no God.* (Harkavy
> Translation)

For thy Maker is thine husband; the LORD of hosts is his name; and thy Redeemer the Holy One of Israel; The God [Elokim] of the whole earth shall he be called.

First, in this verse *HaShem* presents Himself as Israel's *Maker* who is Israel's *husband*. What becomes interesting is that both *Maker* and *Husband* are plural making it literally your Maker<u>s</u> are your Husband<u>s</u>. Also you have the *L-RD* who is the King of Israel and you have His redeemer the *L-RD* of hosts, two *L-RD*s.

There are four passages that show *Elokim/HaShem* referencing Himself with the plural first person pronoun. Let me list them for you:

Genesis 1:26 – *Elokim (plural) says, Let* **us** *make man in* **our** *image and after* **our** *Likeness.*

Genesis 3:22 – *Yahweh [HaShem] Elokim (singular and plural) says, They have become one of* **us**, *knowing good and evil.*

Genesis 11:7 – *Yahweh [HaShem] singular) says, Let* **us** *go down and confound their language.*

Isaiah 6:8 – *Adhonai (plural) says, Who will I send and who will go for* **us**?

Notice each one of these passages contains a major word for G-d, and one contains the combination of two of them: *Elokim, Yahweh Elokim, Yahweh* and *Adhonai*. What is the literal meaning? Rabbinic Judaism goes to great lengths to get around what the Author of language Himself says. Why can't they take *Elokim/Yahweh* at His own Word? He is referring to Himself in the plural as a plural unity of one (*echad*).

Go back to the word *Yahweh* or the *L-RD* in Genesis 11:7. Rabbinic Judaism wants to insert an interpretation that is not in the text by making the plural *us* for the *L-RD* to refer to angels. They also attempt the same argument in Genesis 1:26; however, there are again no angels in the context. The literal explanation is that the *L-RD* spoke in the plural using a plural first person pronoun for Himself. It is the same word used in verses 3 through 4 when the people say, *let us make bricks*, and *let us build us a city*, and *let us make us a name lest we be scattered.* Everyone says that when the people used the term *us* they were speaking in the plural, but when G-d uses it rabbinic Judaism says, "Oh no, it does not mean that G-d is plural; it is speaking of angels." Isn't it arrogant on man's part when the *L-RD* wrote something very simple to understand, that finite man is telling the *L-RD* that this is not what He meant, because it goes against their preset bias of who the *L-RD* is? As a side note it is interesting that the people at the tower of Babel wanted to make a name for themselves. In their disobedience to *HaShem*'s command to scatter and populate the earth, they stayed and were judged. However, in Genesis 12:2 the *L-RD* said to Abraham in the first statement of the Abrahamic Covenant *I will bless you, and make your name great*, because Abraham obeyed.

Because rabbinic Judaism focuses on the absolute oneness (*yachid*) of *Elokim* they have refused to see what *Elokim* (the *L-RD*) literally had Moses and the Prophets record concerning Himself.

Chapter Four:
Audible and/or Visible
Appearances of Elokim and
Yahweh

Theophanies are a subject that rabbinic Judaism clearly saw. But again if you come to the text with a set bias and the text differs from that bias, then how do you deal with it? Often people will reinterpret it to fit their bias. Rabbis, priests and preachers all have a tendency to do that. However, if you are consistent with the literal method of interpretation that I referred to in chapter two, you will not let your bias override what *HaShem* has said. Following this rule makes us listen to *HaShem* and not to our prejudices or biases.

The term *theophany* is not a biblical term. It comes from two Greek words, and it means *theos* (G-d) and *phaino* (shine, give light), but in the passive the verb means "to appear or to be revealed." So in the *Tanakh* you have times when G-d either appeared and/or spoke audibly to man. These can be very difficult and impossible to understand with a rabbinic belief that *Elokim* cannot take on the form of a man to interact with man. As we read the *Tanakh* we find that *HaShem* has appeared to man using other names or titles such as *the angel of the LORD*, *the Captain of the LORD's host*. What we find is that the names *L-RD*, *Elokim*, *angel of the LORD* [*HaShem*], as well as *Shechinah* are used interchangeably. *Shechinah* is a term to indicate the very presence of *Elokim* Himself as when He dwelt in the Tabernacle and Solomon's Temple. But there is another surprising factor that we will illustrate shortly. *The angel of the LORD* is used interchangeably with *L-RD*, and *Elokim*, and *the angel of the L-RD* claims deity and equality with the *L-RD*.

Exodus 3:1-17 ... Angel of HaShem

Let us look at one of the most well-known passages in Judaism, found in Exodus 3:1-15, with the call of Moses.

¹ Now Moses kept the flock of Jethro his father in law, the priest of Midian: and he led the flock to the backside of the desert, and came to the mount of God, even to Horeb [Mt. Sinai].

² And the **angel of the LORD appeared** *unto him in a* **flame of fire** *out of the midst of a bush: and he looked, and, behold, the bush burned with fire, and the bush was not consumed.*

³ And Moses said, I will now turn aside, and see this great sight, why the bush is not burnt.

⁴ And when the **LORD** [*HaShem*] *saw that he turned aside to see,* **God** [*Elokim*] *called unto him out of the midst of the bush, and said, Moses, Moses, and he said, Here am I.*

⁵ And he said, **Draw not nigh hither: put off thy shoes from off they feet, for the place whereon you are standing is holy ground.**

⁶ Moreover he said, **I am the God** [*Elohim*] *of thy father, the God of* **Abraham***, the God of* **Isaac***, and the God of* **Jacob***. And Moses hid his face for he was afraid to look upon God* [*Elohim*]. *⁷ And the* **LORD** [*HaShem*] **said** *I have surely seen the* *affliction of* **my people** *which are in Egypt, and have heard their cry by reason of their taskmasters; for I know their sorrow;*

[8] *And* **I am come down to deliver them** *out of the hand of the Egyptians, and* **to bring them up out of that land** *unto a good land and a large, unto a land flowing with milk and honey; unto the place of the Canaanites, and the Hittites, and the Amorites, and the Perizzites, and the Hivites, and the Jebusites.*

[9] *Now therefore, behold, the cry of the children of Israel is come unto me and I have also seen the oppression wherewith the Egyptians oppress them.*

[10] *Come now therefore, and I will send you unto Pharaoh, that thou mayest bring forth* **my people** *the children of Israel out of Egypt.*

[11] *And Moses said unto* **God** *[Elokim] Who am I, that I should go unto Pharaoh, and that I should bring forth the children of Israel out of Egypt?*

[12] *And he said, certainly I will be with you; and this shall be a token unto you, that I have sent you: When thou hast brought forth the people out of Egypt, you shall serve God [Elokim] upon this mountain.*

[13] *And Moses said unto* **God** *[Elokim], Behold, when I come unto the children of Israel, and shall say unto them, The God [Elokim] of your fathers hath sent me unto you; and they shall say to me, What is his name? what shall I say unto them?*

[14] **And God** *[Elokim] said unto Moses,* **I AM THAT I AM**: *and he said Thus shalt you say unto the children of Israel,* **I AM hath sent me unto you**.

[15] *And* **God** *[Elokim] said moreover unto Moses, Thus shalt you say unto the children of Israel, The* **LORD God** *[Yahweh Elokim]* **of your fathers**, **the**

God [*Elokim*] of Abraham, the God [*Elokim*] of Isaac, *and* the God [*Elokim*] of Jacob, *hath sent me unto you: this is* **my name** *for ever, and this is my memorial unto all generations.*

[16] *Go, and gather the elders of Israel together, and say unto them,* **The** *Lord* **God of your fathers,** *the* **God of Abraham, of Isaac, and of Jacob, appeared unto me [Moses],** *saying,* **I** *have surely visited you, and seen that which is done to you in Egypt:*

[17] *And* **I** *have said,* **I will bring you up out of the affliction of Egypt** *unto the land of the Canaanites, and the Hittites, and the Amorites, and the Perizzites, and the Hivites, and the Jebusites, unto a land flowing with milk and honey.*

I quoted the whole passage and have **bolded** some key points because there are several things that we need to understand what *Elokim* is literally saying. Notice the points:

- Verse 2 - The speaker is *the angel of the LORD* who is also the *Shechinah* which is the very presence of G-d.

- Verse 4 - The *L-RD* saw and *Elokim* called.

- Verse 6 - The speaker identifies Himself as the *Elokim* of Abraham, Isaac and Jacob.

- Verse 7 - The *L-RD* speaks and calls Israel my people.

- Verse 9 - Israel's cry has come unto *me*.

- Verse 10 – *The L-RD* says I will send you to *my people.*

- Verse 12 - You are to serve *Elokim* later on this mountain.

- Verse 14 - He is the *I AM THAT I AM*, the *Shechinah* that is sending Moses. That literally means that He is the eternally present G-d.

- Verse 15 - *Elokim* said and identifies Himself as the L-RD [*Yahweh*] G-d [*Elokim*]. Again it is a combination of plural and singular names for G-d.

- Verse 16 - The *L-RD* who appeared to Abraham, Isaac and Jacob has appeared to Moses. Compare with Genesis 12:7; 17:1, 22; 18:1; 26:2-4; 28:13-14.

- Verse 17 - He will bring them from Egypt to the Promised Land flowing with milk and honey. That would be in partial fulfillment of the covenant to Abraham. Compare with Judges 2:1 then Genesis 15:1, 2, 17-18.

Notice how the names of G-d are used interchangeably. The *Shechinah* and *the angel of the LORD* are also part of the combination of terms used by G-d as He spoke to Moses in the burning bush.

Rabbinic Judaism likes to say that the *angel of the LORD* is speaking as a representative of G-d, meaning that the angel himself is a created being. In the text the word angel means Messenger. If what rabbinic Judaism says is true, since when does a created being receive worship and require a human to remove his shoes because he is standing on holy ground? Created beings do not receive worship nor do they claim holiness that alone belongs to *HaShem*. So who is *the angel of the LORD* that appeared unto Moses?

As we go on we find that *the angel of the LORD* is *HaShem* and yet distinct from *HaShem* because He is a

41

plurality in unity. To be exact, He (*the angel of the LORD*) is the Second Person of the Plural unity of *Elokim*.

Let us continue by looking at Genesis 22 in connection with father Abraham. First, in Genesis 12:7 and 17:1, *HaShem* appears to Abraham and the word *appears* means a physical manifestation. The proof of a physical appearance is then in 17:22; when the *L-RD* and Abraham are finished talking, the text states *and God* [*Elokim*] *went up from Abraham*, or in other words *Elokim* ascended up from Abraham's presence.

Genesis 22 ... The Angel of HaShem

Now look at portions of Genesis 22 as we identify who is testing Abraham:

¹ And it came to pass after these things, that **God** [*Elokim*] *did tempt Abraham, and said unto him, Abraham: and he said, Behold here I am.*
² And he said, Take now thy son, thine only son Isaac, whom thou lovest, and get thee into the land of Moriah: and offer him there for a burnt-offering upon one of the mountains which I will tell you.
¹⁰ And Abraham stretched forth his hand, and took the knife to slay his son.
¹¹ And **the angel of the** ***LORD*** **called unto him** *out of heaven, and said, Abraham, Abraham: and he said, Here am I.*
¹² And he said, lay not thine hand upon the lad, neither do thou any thing unto him: **for now I know that thou fearest God** [*Elokim*]*, seeing thou has not withheld thy son,* **thine only son from me***.*
¹⁵ And **the angel of the** ***LORD*** **called** *unto Abraham out of heaven the second time,*

¹⁶ And said, **By myself I have sworn, saith the** **LORD** *[HaShem], for because thou has done this thing, and has not withheld thy son, thine only son.*

¹⁷ That in blessing **I will bless you**, *and in multiplying* **I will multiply thy seed as the stars of heaven**, *and* **as the sand which is upon the sea shore**; *and thy seed shall posses the gate of his enemies.*

¹⁸ And in thy seed shall all the nations of the earth be blessed; because thou has **obeyed my voice**.

In Genesis 22 *Elokim* tests Abraham by asking him to offer his only (*yachid*) son Isaac. Abraham complies, and then in verse 11 *the angel of the LORD* calls to him out of heaven and says, *now I know* that you fear *Elokim* since you did not withhold your *only son from me*, and that is *the angel of the LORD* speaking as *HaShem* Himself. Then in verses 15 through 16 it is *the angel of the LORD* who makes an oath and a promise to Abraham because *my voice* was obeyed. This cannot be a created being, but He has to be *HaShem* Himself. *HaShem, Elokim* as *the angel of the LORD* tested Abraham's faith in Him to see if he would obey His command. Then He says *by myself I have sworn* and repeats promises that He said in Genesis 15:5. *The angel of the LORD* is distinct from and yet equal to the *L-RD, HaShem,* because He is a plurality in unity, the Second Person of the plural unity of *Elokim*.

Exodus 23:20-23 ... The Angel

Notice in Exodus 23:20-23, another significant passage, where the *L-RD* or *HaShem* combines the plural *Elokim* with the singular *L-RD*. He is finishing His instructions to Moses, that He started back in Exodus 20:1 with the giving of the

Law of Moses, which includes the 10 commandments. Notice how *Elokim* begins in Exodus 20:1-2:

> [1] *And God* [**Elokim**] *spoke all these words, saying,*
> [2] *I am the LORD* [*HaShem*] *thy God* [*Elokim*]*, which have brought you out of the land of Egypt.*

Notice how G-d combines the plural [*Elokim*] and the singular [*L-RD*] aspect of His person. G-d does that 930 times in the *Tanakh*. Notice as well that *the angel of the LORD* said the identical thing in Judges 2:1 which will be quoted shortly.

Now look at Exodus 23:20-23:

> [20] *Behold, I send* **an Angel** *before you, to keep you in the way, and to bring you into the place where I have prepared.*
> [21] **Beware of him***, and* **obey his voice, provoke him not***; for* **he will not pardon your transgressions***: for* **my name is in him**.
> [22] *But if you shall indeed obey* **his voice***, and do all that* **I speak***; then* **I will** *be an enemy unto your enemies, and an adversary unto your adversaries.*
> [23] **For mine Angel** *shall go before you, and bring you in unto the Amorites, and the Hittites, and the Perizzites, and the Canaanites, the Hivites, and the Jebusites: and I will cut them off.*

This *angel* had the ability to forgive sin and the very Name of *HaShem* was in Him. Rabbis of old struggled with this because of the clear distinction between *HaShem* and the *angel*. This *angel* [Messenger] had the attributes of *HaShem* that only *Elokim* could have; to forgive sin and have the Name of *HaShem* in Him. They called Him *Metatron* and even referenced Him to Isaiah 63:9 as the *angel* of

44

HaShem's face. The rabbis saw the clear presentation of the plurality of *Elokim* who is one [*echad*], but rejected it because of their focus on absolute oneness [*yachid*] of *Elokim*.

Joshua 5:13-15 ... Captain of the LORD's Host

In the next presentation of a theophany we have Joshua doing reconnaissance on Jericho when he meets what he thinks is a man of war. In Joshua 5 he quickly finds out who this individual is as verses 13 through 15 record:

> *¹³ And it came to pass, when Joshua was by Jericho that he lifted up his eyes and looked, and, behold, there stood* **a man** *over against him with his sword drawn in his hand: and Joshua went unto him, and said unto him, Art thou for us, or for our adversaries?*
> *¹⁴ And he said, Nay; but as* **captain of the host of the LORD** *am I now come and* **Joshua fell on his face** *to the earth, and* **did worship** *and said unto him, What say my lord unto his servant?*
> *¹⁵ And the captain of the LORD's host said unto Joshua,* **Loose thy shoe from off thy foot: for the place whereon thou standest is holy**. *And Joshua did so.* [Emphasis is mine.]

Notice Joshua's response when the Captain of the *L-RD*'s host identified Himself; he fell down and worshipped Him. To worship a man as G-d is idolatry, but this Captain appeared as a man, yet He spoke as *HaShem* for He then tells Joshua to remove his shoes because this is holy ground. As with Moses (Exodus 3:2-7) we have a Messenger of the *L-RD* receiving worship which only *Elokim*, and *L-RD* or

HaShem can receive. Again here is a direct reference to the plurality of **HaShem Elokim, two of the main names for G-d;** yet He is one (*echad*).

Here is an interesting question to consider: If *HaShem Elokim* appeared in human form to Abraham, Moses and now Joshua, is it theologically out of bounds to believe that G-d could come as a man and dwell among us through the incarnation of G-d as Jesus? Moses in Genesis 3:15 and the Prophets (as written in Isaiah 9:6-7 [5-6], Jeremiah 23:5-8, and Daniel 9:24-27) wrote that *HaShem Elokim* would take on flesh and dwell among us.

Judges 2:1 ... The Angel of HaShem

Let us look at one more theophany that shows the plurality of *Elokim* as one (*echad*) and yet He, the Angel of the L-RD, speaks as *HaShem* in Judges 2:1 to Israel:

> *And an angel of the LORD came up from Gilgal to Bochim, and said,* **I made** *you to go up out of Egypt, and have* **brought you unto the land** *which* **I swore unto your fathers**, *and I said,* **I will never break my covenant with you**.

In this passage *the angel of the LORD* speaks to Israel after the victories of Joshua upon entering the Land. The tribal territories have been assigned and they met to hear *the angel of the LORD* speak to them. Notice that He states that He brought Israel out of Egypt unto the Promised Land that *He swore to your fathers*. Who is *He*? He is the speaker at the beginning of verse 1. Who is the speaker? *The angel of the LORD*.

First *He* took Israel from point A (Egypt) to point B (Promised Land) which *He* swore to your fathers. *The angel of the LORD* is referring back to the Abrahamic Covenant, in particular Genesis 15. Who made the covenant with Abraham? The *L-RD*! Yet if you go back to read Genesis 15, there is some information on the identity of *HaShem*. First in Genesis 15 verses 1 and 4, He is called *the word of the LORD* that came and spoke to Abraham, and made or confirmed the covenant by walking between the slain animals. **He** was the *Shechinah*, the very presence of *HaShem* who is also called the *Word* that made the covenant.[21] Abraham was not allowed to participate in the making of the covenant. The *Word, HaShem,* (as well as the *Shechinah*), made it and swore by Himself that He was going to do this. That is what *the angel of the LORD* is referring to in Judges 2:1.

Also *the angel of the LORD* is the same *angel* that Moses spoke of in Exodus 23:20-23 and 33:1-2. **He** is the one who could forgive their transgressions and had the very Name of the *L-RD* in Him which again belongs to *HaShem* alone.

We saw that *the angel of the LORD* connected Himself with *the word of the LORD* that spoke to Abraham. It is recorded in 1 Samuel 3:21 that Samuel the Prophet knew *HaShem* by *the word of the LORD* that revealed Himself and spoke to him. The Psalmist in Psalm 33:6 also understood that *the word of the LORD* was a person when he said:

By the word of the LORD were the heavens made; and all the host of them by the breath of **his** mouth.

Notice that the creator of Genesis 1 spoke by *the word of the LORD* when He created by *the breath of His mouth*. The

---

[21] See the New Testament, Gospel of John 1:1-3, Revelation 19:11-14.

word of the LORD is a person; He again is the Second Person of *Elokim.* Genesis 1:3, 6, 9, 11, 14, 20, 24 and 26 taken together clearly states that He spoke, and everything in six literal 24-hour days was created by Him.[22] Even Elijah the prophet knew *the word of the LORD* because he spoke with Him in 1 Kings 19:9-18. Here *the word of the LORD* that spoke to Elijah is identified as the *L-RD* or *HaShem.*

Exodus 14:15-28 ... Shechinah Pillar of Cloud and Fire

The *Shechinah* glory, the very presence of the *L-RD* or *HaShem,* is recognized by three features: cloud, smoke and fire. The *Shechinah* is also connected to *the angel of the LORD* who spoke and acted as *HaShem* in protecting Israel, blessing Israel and also judging Israel when they sinned against Him. In a careful study of those passages cited in this chapter regarding the theophanies of *Elokim* it becomes clear that the very presence of *HaShem* as the *Shechinah* shows the plurality of *HaShem.* G-d's Word reveals that He (*HaShem*) is connected with *the angel of the LORD* and *Elokim.*

In Exodus 14, the Egyptian army is attacking Israel as the people stood at the Red Sea. In verse 15 *HaShem* spoke to Moses, then in verse 19 *the angel of God* [*Elokim*] is connected to the *Shechinah* presence of *HaShem*, removed and went behind them to separate Israel and the Egyptians. The cloud became darkness on the Egyptian side and light for Israel. Then in verse 24 notice that regarding the same cloud that is connected to *the angel of God* and the *Shechinah* presence, the text states the following:

---

[22] See the New Testament Gospel of John 1:1-3, 10; and the Epistle to the Colossians 1:15-18; 2:9.

48

And it came to pass, that in the morning watch the **LORD** *looked unto the host of the Egyptians* **through the pillar of fire** *and* **of the cloud***, and troubled the host of the Egyptians.*

Once again you have the *L-RD* or *HaShem, the angel of God,* who in this case is the *Shechinah* presence of *HaShem,* being used interchangeably in the text. *The angel of God* in the text is made equal to *HaShem* once again showing that the Second Person of the plural unity of *Elokim* and the *L-RD* is one [*echad*].

The angel of the LORD and the *Shechinah* glory of the *L-RD* are presented together as being equal and yet distinct from *HaShem.* Observe the following points:

- The *Shechinah* glory of Genesis 15:17 and the Word of the *L-RD* are connected together in Genesis 15:1 and 4 as the *angel of the LORD* in Judges 2:1.

- The *Shechinah* glory, *Elokim* and the *L-RD* are connected together in Exodus 3.

- In Exodus 20-23 as well as Exodus 32, the *L-RD* or *HaShem* appears as the *Shechinah* glory as the Law is given and as the angel [Messenger] with the Name of G-d in Him.

- The *Shechinah* glory appears at the Tent of Meeting in the wilderness in Exodus 33:7-11 and gives instruction to Moses in Exodus 24:15-18.

- The *Shechinah* glory is the one who filled the Tabernacle in Exodus 40:34-35.

- It is the *Shechinah* glory who judged Nadab and Abihu in Leviticus 9:23-10:2 for offering strange fire before *HaShem.*

- It is the *Shechinah* glory who met with Aaron and Miriam at the door of the Tabernacle in Numbers 12:5 and judged Miriam.

All of these passages show that the *L-RD* is one, yet He is also a plurality of persons each functioning in a unity of one [*echad*]. The *Shechinah* glory and *the angel of the LORD* are visible appearances of the Second Person of *Elokim* before mankind.

As we reviewed the names of G-d we observed two primary things. First, G-d used both plural and singular words to describe Himself. Secondly, *the angel of the LORD* acted as a separate person from the Father, yet they are one [*echad*].

Chapter Five:
Plural Descriptions

Beginning in chapter three, we observed how *Elokim* identified Himself using a plural noun with a singular verb to demonstrate that He is a plurality in one [*echad*], *Elokim*. There are four exceptions to that pattern that *Elokim* uses in identifying Himself to His people, and these are discussed below.

Plural Verbs

In these four exceptions, the *Elokim* of Abraham, Jacob, David and the Psalmist used the plural verb with the plural noun *Elokim*. Even though this is correct grammar *Elokim* consistency chose to use the singular verb as His pattern of expressing His being to Israel. So the plural noun and the singular verb should draw our attention to what He is saying. When He uses the plural noun with a plural verb it equally should draw our attention because it is not His normal usage. Let us look at the references where this happens in the context of Abraham and King Abimelech in Genesis 20:13:

> *And it came to pass, when God caused me to wander from my father's house, that I said unto her* [Sarah], *This is your kindness which you shall show unto me; at every place whither we shall come, say of me, He is my brother.*

In the English translations it is not translated as it is written in the Hebrew. In the Hebrew it literal says: "*God* [*Elokim*] **they** *caused me to wander…*" Abraham referred to

Elokim in the plural and not singular. The next usage occurs in Genesis 35:7 in connection to Jacob:

> *There he built an altar and named the site El-bethel,*
> *for it was there that God had revealed Himself to*
> *him when he was fleeing from his brother.* (Jewish
> Study Bible)

Once again if it is translated literally as the Hebrew text states, Jacob said: "...*God [Elokim] revealed* **themselves**...." So Abraham and Jacob both referred to *Elokim* in the plural. Next we have David, who is worshipping the L-RD G-d [*HaShem Elokim*] for what had just been revealed to Him through the prophet Nathan in 2 Samuel 7:23 concerning the Davidic Covenant, saying:

> *And what one nation in the earth is like your people,*
> *even like Israel, whom God went to redeem for a*
> *people to himself, ...*

Likewise when this praise of the Psalmist is literally translated it is also in the plural for it states: "*whom God [Elokim] they redeemed for* **themselves**,...." These verses are uniquely showing the plurality of *Elokim* by Abraham, Jacob and now David the Psalmist. The L-RD of creation is being shown as a plurality in unity, plural yet one [*echad*] just as Genesis 1:1 and 26 record. One final verse from Psalm 58:11[12] as the unknown psalmist writes:

> *Men will say, "There is, then, a reward for the*
> *righteous; there is indeed, divine* justice on earth.

The unknown psalmist is literally saying, when the passage is translated word for word, that *God* [*Elokim*] **they** *judge on earth.*

Only when we embrace these plural descriptions along with how *Elokim*, the L-RD [*HaShem*], *the angel of the LORD,* and the Captain of the L-RD's host have represented Themselves to Israel through the centuries can we be faithful to the Word of *HaShem*. Yet in rabbinic Judaism, Jewish people are told to study *Mishnah* and *Talmud* over the Word of *HaShem*.

Plural Descriptions

Yet even what we have discussed so far is not all inclusive, for there are other plural descriptions of the G-d of Israel in His Word. Look together with me at Psalm 149:2a:

> *Let Israel rejoice in its maker;...*

In the Hebrew the word for *maker* is plural, and it literally reads, *let Israel rejoice in its maker*s. This is a continued reaffirmation of Genesis 1 when *Elokim* created the universe and the earth as one [*echad*] *Elokim*, but plural. Another interesting verse comes from Solomon in Ecclesiastes 12:1, which states:

> *Remember now your Creator in the days of your youth, ...*

Here the plural description again relates to *Elokim* who created mankind. The word *Creator* in Hebrew is also in the plural and literally says *remember now your Creator*s *in the days of your youth*, which again corresponds with the plurality that G-d set forth of Himself in Genesis 1 and many other passages that we have looked at.

The Book of Isaiah makes you breathless as you read from beginning to end of the nature and essence of *HaShem* of Israel. In Isaiah 48:12-13, 16 there is absolutely a stunning verse on the Person of *HaShem* as He spoke to Israel:

> [12] *Hearken unto me,* **O Jacob and Israel, my called***:*
> *I am he;* **I am the first***,* **I also am the last***.*
> [13] **Mine hand also has laid the foundation** *of the earth, and* **my right hand has spanned** *the heavens: when I call unto them, they stand up together.*
> [16] *Come near to me, hear this; I have not spoken in secret from the beginning from the time that it was there am I:* **and now the** *Lord* **God, and his Spirit, hath sent me***.* [Emphasis is mine.]

As you read this passage it is *HaShem* who says to Israel, I called you; I called you in Abraham and set you apart to be my people. He continues by speaking of His eternality by stating that He is *the first* and *the last*, He is eternally present. That is what He said to Moses in Exodus 3:14, *I AM THAT I AM*. Remembering back to that passage it was *the angel of the LORD* who spoke to Moses from the burning bush, and He used the words *Elokim* and L-RD [*HaShem*] interchangeably in revealing Himself to Moses. Moses worshipped and removed His shoes because it was holy ground for the *Shechinah* glory of *Elokim* was present. Then in verse 13 of Isaiah 48 He also states that He is the *Creator*. Then look at verse 16 and read it thoughtfully and see His words: a*nd now the Lord God, and his Spirit, hath sent me*. Who is *me* according to the context? It is the speaker who has been talking to Israel in verses 12 through 16. *Me* is the one who called Israel and Jacob; He is the eternal present G-d who is the *Creator* of the universe. This one is the Sent One in verse 16, but notice who sent Him: the L-rd G-d and His Spirit. Here in the *Tanakh*, Isaiah references the plurality of *HaShem* as a tri-unity. To coin my own word *Hakadosh Shilush-Echad* [the Holy Three in

54

One], meaning that the one G-d of Israel is revealed in the Hebrew Scriptures as a plural unity in one. The One who is sent, was sent by the L-rd G-d and His Spirit. When was this One sent? We will see that later as we continue. According to Genesis 1:26, we see that *Elokim,* who created, was plural, a plural unity, and if we study carefully that one of the persons of *Elokim* who consistently became visible in revealing the Father to His people, the evidence points to Him as the Sent One of Isaiah 48:12-16.[23]

In our next passage Isaiah brings an amazing picture to the minds of his readers. In fact from a rabbinic Judaism perspective, this is an impossibility. It cannot happen, nor is it even conceivable. Look with me at Isaiah 50:1, 4-6 and see Isaiah's astonishing statement:

*[1] Thus saith the **LORD**: ...*
*[4] The **Lord** **GOD** **gave me** the tongue of the learned, that I should know how to speak a word in season to him that is weary, he awakened morning by morning, he awakened mine ear to hear as the learned.*
[5] The Lord GOD opened my ear, and I was not rebellious, neither turned away back.
*[6] I gave **my** back to the smiters, and **my** cheeks to them that plucked off the hair: I hid not **my** face from shame and spitting.*

First, verse one will identify our speaker, who is the L-RD or *HaShem.* If you follow the "I" through verses 1-3 you will

---

[23] See the following passages in the New Testament Gospel of John for the identity of the Sent One: 3:17, 34; 4:34; 5:23-24, 30, 36-38; 6:29, 38-40, 44, 57; 7:16, 18, 28-29, 33; 8:16, 18, 26, 29, 42; 9:4; 10:36; 11:42; 12:44-45, 49; 13:16, 20; 14:24; 15:21; 16:5; 17:3, 8, 18, 21, 23, 25; 20:21.

see that the speaker has not changed, for the personal pronoun "I" referring to the speaker is abundant. Then we come to verse 4 and it says, *The Lord God gave me.* Once again who is *me*? [Here the speaker changes pronouns, from *I* to *me*.] The *me* would be the speaker from verse one, *HaShem*. Who then is the L-rd G-d in verse 4 who gives something to *HaShem*? This is another example of the plurality of *Elokim*, yet here it is the L-RD, *HaShem*, who is speaking and referencing the **L-rd G-d.** There are two personalities here: the L-RD [*HaShem*] and the **L-rd G-d,** who would be G-d the Father, the First Person of the plurality of G-d. We see that the L-rd G-d awakens *HaShem* for Him to learn as a disciple. As a side thought, since when does *HaShem* need to learn anything? Since when does *HaShem* sleep that He needs to be awakened? *HaShem* was not rebellious in verse 5. Then in verse 6 there is an unbelievable statement concerning *HaShem*. Let me quote it again and look at the personal pronouns that refer back to the speaker of verse 1, *HaShem*:

> **I** *gave* **my** *back to the smiters, and* **my** *cheeks to them that plucked off the hair:* **I** *hid not* **my** *face from shame and spitting.*

Here *HaShem* says that He gave (a voluntary act) His back to the smiters, as well as His face to those who would pull out His beard. He did not hide His face from those spitting at Him, bringing Him to open shame. Does *HaShem* have a back, cheeks and beard? Of course not, for He is Spirit and not human. So how could this possibly happen—unless in the prophetic future *HaShem* became a man? That is the unthinkable, and yet that is exact what *HaShem* says of Himself: He became a man! We see not a man becoming G-d, but G-d becoming a Man. These acts that *HaShem* says were committed against Him could only have happened to

Him if He became a human being.[24] Did *HaShem* take on
flesh and dwell among us?[25] That is what the L-RD is saying
through the pen of Isaiah. When did that happen? Through
the virgin birth (Isaiah 7:14) of the Messiah and when
HaShem gave His son (Isaiah 9:6-7 [5-6]).[26]

Let us once again look at the prophet Isaiah as he
continues to show plural descriptions of *HaShem*. He
records the following in Isaiah 54:5 where He states:

> *For your* **Maker** *is your* **husband***; the LORD of
> hosts is his name; and your Redeemer the Holy One
> of Israel; The God of the whole earth shall he be
> called.*

Isaiah continues to say things that are hard to digest. There
are two points in this verse: First, the words *maker* and
husband in the Hebrew are plural adjectives. What does that
do to the meaning of the text? It would literally be translated
as your *Makers* are your *Husbands*. Isaiah continues to
repeat the plurality of *Elokim* from Genesis 1 as Scripture
adds one passage upon another in revealing His plurality in
unity [*echad*].   Israel is the wife of *HaShem*, Israel's
Husband, who divorced her because of her sins against Him
in worshipping other gods. Hosea and Jeremiah speak to this
divorce (Hosea 1:9; Jeremiah 3:18), but in the future there
will be a remarriage with complete union and harmony
between Israel and *HaShem* (Jeremiah 31:31-37).

---

[24] See the New Testament Gospel of Matthew 26:67; 27:26, 30;
John 18:22; 19:2-3.
[25] See the New Testament Gospel of John 1:14
[26] See the New Testament Gospels of Matthew 1:1-25 and Luke
1:26-35.

The second point is that we see in Isaiah 54:5 a description of two individuals, one is *the LORD of hosts is my name*, and second *your Redeemer the Holy One of Israel*. This verse is packed with a lot of spiritual things to digest.

One more passage in Isaiah comes from a Servant of the L-RD passage in Isaiah 61:1-2a which states:

> *¹ The Spirit of the Lord GOD is upon* **me***, because the LORD has anointed* **me** *to preach good tidings unto the meek; he hath* **sent me** *to bind up the brokenhearted, to proclaim liberty to the captives, and the opening of the prison to them that are bound;*
> *² To proclaim the acceptable year of the LORD ....*[27]

Here the identity of the Servant of the L-RD has been clearly recognized as a Messianic passage from the *Tanakh* by the sages. The Servant of the L-RD clearly states that the Spirit of the L-rd G-d is on Him, the Messiah, He has been anointed and He has been sent to accomplish a task. This one is the Sent One of the L-rd G-d just as it is recorded in Isaiah 48:16. Isaiah 50 states that the L-RD allowed voluntarily an act of aggression against Him and He received that act willingly in a body of flesh. There is a principle in understanding Scripture that Scripture will interpret Scripture. The problem that has arisen is that rabbis, priests and preachers have often tried to interpret based on their preconceived bias as to what they think a passage should mean instead of interpreting it as *HaShem* Himself gave it.

Let us look at one final passage in Isaiah, 63:7-14, where the L-RD gives an account of the plurality of *HaShem*:

---

[27] See the *New Testament Gospel of Luke* 4:16-21.

*[7] I will mention the loving kindnesses of the **LORD**, and the praises of the **LORD**, according to all that the **LORD** hath bestowed on us, and the great goodness toward the house of Israel, which he hath bestowed on them according to his mercies, and according to the multitude of his loving kindnesses.*

[8] For he [LORD] said, surely they are my people, children that will not lie: so he was their Savior.

[9] In all their affliction he was afflicted, and **the angel of his presence saved them***: in his love and in his pity he redeemed them; and he bare* [bore] *them, and carried them all the days of old.*

[10] **But they rebelled, and vexed his holy Spirit***: therefore he was turned to be their enemy, and he fought against them.*

[11] Then he remembered the days of old, Moses, and his people, saying, Where is he that brought them up out of the sea with the shepherd of his flock? Where is he that put his **holy Spirit** *within him?*

[12] That led them by the right hand of Moses with his glorious arm, dividing the water before them, to make himself an everlasting name?

[13] That led them through the deep, as an [a] *horse in the wilderness, that they should not stumble?*

[14] As a beast going down into the valley, the **Spirit of the LORD** *caused him to rest: so did you lead your people, to make yourself a glorious name.*

In this passage you have references to three persons presented as one [*echad*]. You have (1) the L-RD or *HaShem*, (2) *the angel of His presence* (3) and *His Holy Spirit* that has been grieved. If the Spirit is a force or power, how can you grieve it unless the *it* is a *Him*, a person? Rabbinic Judaism has historically taught that the L-RD is an absolute one (*yachid*), but there are too many passages that contradict that as an absolute truth. *HaShem* consistently has presented Himself as one [*echad*], a plurality of one. The next chapter will deal with the statement that all Jewish people are familiar with, the *Sh'ma*.

I have brought to you passage upon passage that affirms the plural unity of *HaShem Elokim* in the *Tanakh* and will continue to do so throughout the pages of this book. Many Jewish people today are atheists, agnostic or completely secular in their worldview. In the quiet of the night do they ever wonder, "Where is our G-d? Is He real or is it all mythology?" The only way for one to find out is to study and search the Hebrew Bible for oneself and discover the richness of the Faithfulness of the G-d of your fathers Abraham, Isaac and Jacob. Understand that He loves you so very much. He does not want to be eclipsed from His people, but He has been rejected and spurned by the very ones He gave birth to as a nation. Find out for yourself, from Him in His Word why He, G-d, is in Eclipse from the people who are the apple of His eye (Zechariah 2:8) and the ones He has [en]*graven* upon His hands (Isaiah 49:16).

Chapter Six: *The Sh'ma*

A Matter of Full-Hearted Love

I approach this passage with much respect and awe for the Holy One of Israel. The *Sh'ma* of Deuteronomy 6:4-9 incorporates three basic points:

- The oneness of the L-RD—vs. 4

- Our heart-response to the L-RD—vs. 5

- How we are to raise up our children—vs. 6-9

We will focus on verses 4 and 5. Before we go to verse 4, this well-known verse among Jewish people found in the *Torah* (the five books of Moses), let us look at verse 5, which if it is not obeyed makes the rest of the *Sh'ma* irrelevant:

> *And you shall love the LORD thy God with all your heart, and with all your soul, and with all your might.*

Notice the primary focus of the *Sh'ma* is on the heart. The first emphasis is given to the heart because the center of our being is clearly referred to in Scripture as the heart; the soul and might are the responses of the heart. According to Exodus 24:3-4, Israel committed themselves—their hearts—to all that Moses wrote down:

> *³ And Moses came and told the people all the words of the LORD, and all the judgments: and all the*

people answered with one [echad] voice, and said,
All the words which the LORD hath said will we do.
⁴ And Moses wrote all the words of the LORD, ...

On that day the Jewish people committed themselves to keep the Written Law from the *L-RD* as presented to them by Moses. The emphasis in the *Sh'ma* is on doing so with one's *heart*, mind/*soul* and *might*. The *Tanakh* records the checkered history of Israel's lapses in worship of the one true G-d and the times of disobedience. The *Tanakh* also records the many times *HaShem* delivered them, and the judgments they suffered due to being stiff-necked (not bowing to G-d: Exodus 32:9; 33:3, 5; 34:9;) and a hardened hearted (not responding to *HaShem*: I Kings 17:14; Nehemiah 9:16-17, 29; Psalm 95:8-11; Jeremiah 7:26; 19:15). The Assyrian captivity was G-d's judgment of the 10 northern tribes of Israel for corrupting the true worship of G-d with idolatry and images, such as the golden calf. They then compounded their sin with the worship of Baal as recorded in I and II Kings, which describes the spiritual battle between wicked King Ahab and the prophet Elijah; the prophet Hosea also describes their spiritual adultery while the prophet Amos wrote concerning Israel's flagrant violations of the Written Law of Moses. The Babylonian captivity was G-d's judgment against the southern kingdom of Judah for corrupting the true worship of G-d with mere religious observance compounded with idolatry, as recorded in Ezekiel and Jeremiah. The other prophets like Isaiah and Micah also point to Judah's flagrant violations of the Written Law of Moses.

Rabbis of the past have layered man-made rules and regulations upon the Law of G-d with the original intent to clarify how to obey, and make a hedge, or fence around the law to prevent unintentional infractions. While

62

understandable, given the seriousness of breaking instead of observing the law, the addition of many teachings and traditions to the Written Law made it easier to observe the law from a legalistic standpoint but not necessarily from the heart. The *Sh'ma* stands in contrast as calling for a whole-hearted commitment, rather than a legalistic approach, to worshipping and obeying G-d. Indeed, answering the call to worship G-d alone in spirit and reality would naturally require commitment of all one's *heart*, mind and strength, as compared to following a form of religion. This is nothing new and continues to be a challenge for the faithful then as now.

The Oral Law versus the Written Law

When did the Oral Law come into being? How did a body of teachings and traditions grow up alongside the *Tanakh*, even outranking at times the clear words of *HaShem*? It started with the generation after Ezra the Scribe in the School of the *Sophrim* (Scribes) and not with Moses at Mt. Sinai. The Oral Law was not present in the days of the prophet Hosea who refers to Israel as counting the Written Law as a strange thing (as something that does not concern them) (Hosea 8:12). As the Oral Law developed over the centuries, Israel's teachers led the people to believe that the keeping of rabbinic law gave more merit than keeping the very Law of G-d. They usually do not say that directly, but it is recorded in the *Talmud*, which I have quoted earlier beginning on page 32 of this work, as well from my personal copy of *The Chumash*.[28] In all practicality that is what happened.

---

[28] Rabbi Nosson Scherman, *The Chumash*: The *Torah*: *Haftarot and five Megillot* (Brooklyn, NY: Mesorah Publications, 1993), xix, xxiii-xxv.

There are several convincing arguments that address the complete lack of evidence of an Oral Law being handed down through Moses:[29]

- **An oxymoron:** It would have taken a supernatural act to preserve the Oral Law intact for over 1,600 years. If it had been possible to maintain the Oral Law with perfect accuracy, for that long why would it have been necessary to write it down in 200 CE when Judah *Ha-Nasi* first put it to writing?

- **Lost and Found:** During the reign of Manasseh (55 years) the Scriptures had fallen into disuse and the Scriptures were lost from public view. Then under the reign of King Josiah, the grandson of Manasseh the Written Law was rediscovered in the temple, and for decades the celebration of Passover had not been practiced.

> *And Hezekiah sent to all Israel and Judah, and wrote letters also to Ephraim and Manasseh, that they should come to the house of the LORD at Jerusalem, to keep the Passover unto the LORD God of Israel.*
> (2 Chronicles 30:1)

To summarize, and this needs to be thought through carefully. If the Written *Torah* had been lost during the reign of Manasseh and the worship of the G-d of Israel had fallen into such disuse and the temple itself had to be restored in the reign of Josiah (II Chronicles 34) how could the oral memorized

---

[29] Source: Ron Cantor, *Four Proofs There Was No Oral Law*, Published by Messiah's Mandate: Raising Up Leaders for the Coming Israeli Revival, posted at:
http://messiahsmandate.org/four-proofs-there-was-no-oral-torah.

laws, volumes thick, had survived the apostasy of the Kingdom of Judah in those days? That simply is not conceivable. The Written Law could be found and read, but the Oral Law that would have been lost was irretrievable. So if there was any kind of Oral Law it was created by the rabbis sometime after King Josiah, in fact after the captivity itself.

- **All Inclusive Written Law** – The Scriptures carefully record in Exodus 24:3-4 in an emphatic manner that Moses told ALL the people the words of *HaShem* and ALL His judgments, and ALL the people said with one [*echad*] voice that ALL the words of the Law they would do, and Moses wrote down ALL the words of *HaShem*.

    "Everything the LORD has said we will do." Moses then wrote down everything the LORD had said (Exodus 24:3-4a).

    That simply cannot be put more clearly (Deuteronomy 4:2; 12:32; Joshua 1:8; 8:32-35), meaning there is no secret Oral Law from the time of Moses.

The people were commanded to obey the Written Law:

[10] If thou shalt hearken unto the voice of the LORD thy God, to keep his commandments and his statutes which are written in this book of the law, and if thou turn unto the LORD thy God with all thine heart, and with all thy soul. (Deuteronomy 30:10)

The completed book of law, placed in the ark, became a witness against the Israelites, the measure of their faithfulness to the covenant, Deuteronomy 31:24-26.

²⁴ And it came to pass, when Moses had made an end of writing the words of this law in a book, until they were finished,
²⁵ That Moses commanded the Levites, which bare the ark of the covenant of the Lord, saying,
²⁶ Take this book of the law, and put it in the side of the ark of the covenant of the LORD your God, that it may be there for a witness against thee.

In Joshua 1:8, G-d commands Joshua to observe the Written Law in the beginning of the Prophecy section of the *Tanakh*. No mention is made of an Oral Law or tradition.

This book of the law shall not depart out of thy mouth; but thou shalt meditate therein day and night, that thou mayest observe to do according to all that is written therein: for then thou shalt make thy way prosperous, and then thou shalt have good success.

Not only do the Prophets begin with meditating on that which was written, the first chapter of the Writing section of the *Tanakh*, the Psalms, amplifies what *HaShem* said to Joshua. Let us look at Psalm 1, verses 1-2.

¹ Blessed is the man that walketh not in the counsel of the ungodly, nor standeth in the way of sinners, nor sitteth in the seat of the scornful. ² But his delight is in the law of the Lord; and in his law doth he meditate day and night.

The introductions to both the Prophets and the Writings echo the teaching of Moses, that he placed the Written Law as the only Law to be studied and obeyed. According to Deuteronomy 17:18, even the king of Israel was to make his own personal copy of the Written Law of Moses so he could righteously rule and judge the people.

Think of this change of focus from the Written Law to the Oral Law in terms of a troubled marriage: After all, Israel was the wife of *HaShem*. Israel had separated herself from her G-d by idolatry and hardness of heart to *HaShem*'s Law, and *HaShem* in response divorced her. This is not a final position, as we read that *HaShem* will draw Israel back and comfort her and redeem her (Isaiah 40:1-2). Looking at G-d's response from a purely human perspective, what if you as a married person loved another woman or man? Your spouse would be angry and so was *HaShem*. If you completely neglected her or him, your spouse would become indifferent and cold to you and so has *HaShem*. What if you took the words of your spouse and added layers of new meanings to their words that made your spouse's words of lesser value? That is exactly what rabbinic Judaism has done to *HaShem*. Rabbinic Judaism values the writings of rabbis more than the Word of *HaShem*. The words of the rabbis have been given more honor and have been exalted over the words of *HaShem*. Until Israel realizes that rabbinic Judaism has supplanted *HaShem*'s law with a law of rabbinic invention, Israel will suffer the silence, the eclipse of *HaShem*. The body of rabbinic teachings that forms the Oral Law developed through the *Sophrim*, the *Mishnah* and later through Rabbi ben Zakkai in 70 CE, and later still through the *Talmud*. As ears then and today focus primarily on rabbinic teachings and are closed to the words of *HaShem*, the Jewish people in the Land and dispersed throughout the world will continue to experience the silence of *HaShem*. Thus G-d will continue to be eclipsed from His people. Sadly, there is a famine of the Word of *HaShem* today among your people, just as Amos said there would be

67

(Amos 8:11-12). But be encouraged. *HaShem* is very near to you:

> *Therefore say to them, Thus saith the Lord of hosts:*
> *turn you unto me, saith the Lord of hosts, and I will*
> *turn to you, says the Lord of hosts* (Zechariah 1:3).

Although my discussion of rabbinic Judaism sounds very negative, I do not want you to think that I am attacking rabbis personally. I am bringing to your attention what has happened over the centuries. Your rabbis are merely reflecting what they have been taught by their fathers, and what their fathers were taught by their fathers, etc. So they are a product of centuries of teaching that was based on a false assumption, namely that there is an Oral Law that superseded the Written Law given by *HaShem* to Moses, who repeated it supposedly to Joshua, who repeated it to the Judges, and the Judges repeated it to the Prophets and then to the Scribes, the school of the Sophrim.

> *Even from the days of your fathers you are gone*
> *away from mine ordinances and have not kept them.*
> *Return to me, and I will return to you, saith the Lord*
> *of hosts. But you say, 'Wherein shall we return?'*
> (Malachi 3:7)

Going back to the *Sh'ma* in Deuteronomy 6:5, we can ask ourselves, "Has *HaShem* been loved with the whole heart, soul and might, or has rabbinic law been loved and honored?" David loved the Written Law of G-d and instructed his fellow Israeli to do the same as we see in Psalm 37:31 when he said, *The law of his God is in his heart; none of his steps shall slide.* Has rabbinic Judaism drawn G-d's people closer to Him? Jewish people overall have already answered that by turning their backs to rabbinic law and becoming completely secular in all of life responses.

Our G-d Is One –Plural Clues

Now we come to the core of the *Sh'ma* in verse 4 that every Jewish person knows by heart:

Hear, O Israel: The LORD our God is **one** *LORD.*

The focus in this verse is on the word *one*. But let us look at the rest of the verse before we go to the word *one* (*echad*). Throughout this book I have been referencing the word *one* with the words *echad* and *yachid*. Now you will see clearly the distinction between these two terms, which both mean *one*.

First you have the word *L-RD* used twice in verse 4; and as stated in chapter three of this book, it is a singular word for *HaShem*. However, the word G-d in verse 4 is *Elohenu*, and that is the plural form for the singular words *El* or *Eloah*, literally meaning "our G-ds." Then we come to the word *one* or *echad*. This word has been traditionally taught at least since the days of Maimonides and most likely in and before the first century CE by rabbinic Judaism as being an absolute one [*yachid*], meaning G-d is one, G-d standing alone by Himself. Is this true? Do the words of rabbinic Judaism reflect the meaning that *HaShem* used of Himself, or do they reflect rabbinic Judaism's interpretation? Let us look at the background for the word *one*.

Moses Maimonides (1135-1204) wrote the thirteen principles of the Jewish faith. The second principle is:

I believe with perfect faith that G-d is one. There is no unity that is in any way like His. He alone is our G-d—He was, He is, and He will be.

69

However, Maimonides saw something that he believed gave the wrong concept of G-d from his rabbinic perspective. Remember *HaShem* is the author of language and the author of the Hebrew Scriptures. He is perfectly capable of defining Himself without the aid of any man. Maimonides looked at the word *echad*, which is translated in the Hebrew text as *one*. But he did not like the word *HaShem* used, so in his *Principles of Faith* he used another Hebrew word, *yachid*, which also means *one*. But the two words do not mean the same thing even though they both mean one. So rabbinic Judaism today follows the lead of Maimonides, but what did Maimonides see that caused him to not use the word that *HaShem* used of Himself? Again it all goes back to an assumption that *Elokim* is an absolute one [*yachid*].

The word for *one* in the Hebrew text for Deuteronomy 6:4 is אחד or *echad*. There are five principle ways that *echad* is used, but that can be narrowed down to the following three:

- Used as a unity, or compound unity;
- Denotes a context of plurality;
- Individual one among others.

In the writings of Moses the word *echad* is used 382 times, and when you go through each reference you find out what Maimonides saw and why he chose to use another word, יחיד, [*yachid*] in its place, instead of the word *HaShem* chose to use.

As you go through all the references, here is the discovery that most rabbis themselves have never studied. Study this for yourself by getting a Young's Concordance[30]

---

[30] Robert Young, *Young's Analytical Concordance to the Bible* (Grand Rapids, MI: Eerdmans Publishing, 1977).

and searching out each individual reference. First, the minority use of *echad* is that of a compound unity that has the meaning of two or more things coming together as *one*. Let me illustrate with several verses:

> *And God called the light Day and the darkness he called Night. And the evening and the morning were the first [echad] day.* (Genesis 1:5)

> *Therefore shall a man leave his father and his mother, and shall cleave unto his wife: and they shall be one [echad] flesh.* (Genesis 2:24)

> *And Moses came and told the people all the words of the LORD, and all the judgments: and* **all the people answered with one [*echad*]** *voice, and said, All the words which the LORD hath said will we do.* (Exodus 24:3)

> *And they came unto the brook of Eshcol, and cut down from* **thence a branch with one [echad] cluster of grapes**, *and they bare it between two upon a staff and they brought of the pomegranates, and of the figs.* (Numbers 13:23)

In these verses you have two or more things becoming one which is called a compound unity. The *second usage* of a plural context is where you have two or more things referenced and one is selected or chosen out of many, as the follow example illustrates:

> *And he said, take now your son, your only [yachid] son Isaac, whom thou lovest, and get you into the land of Moriah; and offer him there for a burnt offering* **upon one [*echad*] of the mountains** *which I will tell you of.* (Genesis 22:2)

71

But Moses' hands were heavy; and they took a stone, and put it under him and he sat thereon; Aaron and Hur stayed up his hands, **the one** [*echad*] **on the one** [*echad*] **side and the other** [*echad*] **on the other** [*echad*] **side** *and his hands were steady until the going down of the sun.* (Exodus 17:12)

But in the place which the LORD shall choose in **one** [*echad*] **of your tribes,** *there you shall offer your burnt-offerings, and there you shall do all that I command you.* (Deuteronomy 12:14)

One [*echad*] **kid of the goats** *for a sin-offering.* (Numbers 7:52)

Here you will notice that all the references are *one* within the context of many. There were numerous mountains in the area where Abraham was to go, and G-d would show him which *one*. Moses had two arms that Aaron and Hur needed to hold up. Out of the 12 tribes of Israel, G-d would choose *one*. There are many references in Leviticus and Numbers about taking a lamb, goat or bullock to offer before the L-RD. In each one of these cases, where did they go to get a lamb or a goat? The answer is: from a flock of lambs or goats. Where did they go to get a bullock? Again, the answer is obvious: from a herd of bullocks. So even though one is sacrificed, it is necessary to go into a plural context to choose *one* out. This does not mean *one* [*yachid*] *standing alone by itself.* They are each *one* [*echad*] *among others.* I am NOT implying that there is more than one G-d as the pagans do, or that G-d is divisible; He is indivisible. G-d is one in plurality as was explained in chapter one.

The third usage of a plural context is a *cardinal one* where *echad* is used as *one among others*, such as the first day of the week or the first month of the year as illustrated:

72

*In the first month, on the fourteenth day of the month
at even, you shall eat unleavened bread, until the*
one [*echad*] **and twentieth day** *of the month at
even.* (Exodus 12:18)

*And the LORD spoke unto Moses in the wilderness
of Sinai, in the tabernacle of the congregation, on
the* **first** [*echad*] **day of the second month**, *in the
second year after they were come out of the land of
Egypt, saying...* (Numbers 1:1)

These two references mention a specific day or month. Why
does it say on the 21st day or that 1st day? Neither is the only
day of the month; for in the Jewish calendar there are 28
days not just one day; the usage of *echad* here is in the
context of one of many. These and all the other 382
references of *echad* show that Moses never used the word
echad as an absolute one. It is exclusively used within the
context of plurality. So now as we go back to
Deuteronomy 6:4, we can read it again with this
understanding:

Hear O Israel, the LORD [singular] *your God*
[plural] *is one* [*echad*—plural] *LORD* [singular].

The L-RD is one L-RD; there are no other gods. The plural
usage here is in no way meant to suggest that there are others
gods besides *HaShem*. All other gods that man worships are
made up in the minds of man. Isaiah 44:6 is very clear; there
are no other gods besides the L-RD Himself. But as we have
already seen from the Law, Prophets and the Writings,
HaShem references Himself in the plural, yet as *one echad
L-RD*. There is a plurality within *HaShem Elokim*, and that
explains the plural references throughout the *Tanakh*.

One final note on this point: There is a Hebrew word that expresses the concept of *one alone* [*yachid*], standing completely by itself with nothing around it, and that is the word Maimonides liked. Go back to the quote from Genesis 22:2 where the word *yachid* is used in reference to Isaac. G-d designates Isaac the son of promise, as the only son of promise. He and he alone was to be taken and offered before the L-RD. The context of that passage is an absolute *one* and the word *yachid* is used. Yet in the last part of the verse, the word *echad* is used. G-d will show Abraham which one (plural) of the mountains that Abraham was to go to. Maimonides, who believed in the absolute oneness of *HaShem*, saw that *echad* presents the L-RD in a plural context, so he used another word to reflect his interpretation but not *HaShem*'s interpretation. That is what Maimonides saw. One other reference that uses *yachid* is found in Zechariah 12:10 as follows:

I will pour upon the house of David, and upon the inhabitants of Jerusalem, the spirit of grace and of supplications: and they shall look **unto** *me* [for every one] *whom they have pierced and they shall mourn for him, as one* **mourneth** *for his* **only** [yachid] **son***, and shall be in bitterness for him, as one that is in bitterness for his firstborn.*

First I need to deal with two issues in this verse that can be distracting. In the Harkavy Translation here, the words "for every one" are in brackets, which means that those words are not in the original Hebrew text. The second issue is the bold word *unto* in the verse. The word should be *upon me* for that reflects the text. Because the verse looks so much like what happened to Jesus, the Masoretes[31] with their vowel pointings, which are extra-biblical, were able to distract from the real meaning. In this passage, the nation of Israel will weep over Him who is pierced as one weeps over the loss of an only [*yachid*] son. In biblical culture if a widow lost her only [*yachid*] son she not only lost the inheritance but she lost the one who would care for her in the absence of her deceased husband. It was a tragic loss for a widow. Zechariah connects this weeping for a lost son to the one who is pierced, and verse one tells us that the pierced one is *HaShem*, the L-RD. Again as in Isaiah 50 *HaShem* has something happen to Him that could only happen if He came in the flesh and dwelt among us.

As you can see I have stayed with the literal interpretation of the text that I spoke of in chapter three of this book.

I have not departed to the left or to the right, but instead simply sought to understand the Hebrew Scriptures as *HaShem* Himself gave them to you. The *Sh'ma* is a powerful passage, but the existing disconnect with rabbinic Judaism is overlooked. Deuteronomy 6:4 does not match with what has been propagated in Judaism for centuries. I mean no disrespect; I am far more concerned with giving the glory to *HaShem* and honoring Him in the understanding of His Word as He Himself gave it. I challenge you—do not

---

[31] The Masoretes were rabbis of the 10th century CE who added the accent marks to the Hebrew text. Today the Masoretic Text is the foundation of all Bibles both Jewish and Christian. However, the text of Scripture based on the Masoretic Text is predated by other Hebrew Texts, namely the Dead Sea Scrolls and the translation of the Hebrew Text into Greek by 70 rabbis around 250 BCE making that translation over 1,000 years older than the Masoretic Text. The Greek text was called the Septuagint (LXX).

take my word for it; study it out for yourself and let *HaShem* be your Teacher, your Rabbi, and see how He has represented Himself in the *Tanakh*.

So in conclusion when rabbinic Judaism uses Deuteronomy 6:4 to prove absolute oneness of *HaShem*, they do not have the evidence from the *Tanakh* to substantiate it.

Chapter Seven:
Messiah: Seed, King
and Prophet in the Law

I have discovered something refreshing in the last number of years that I would like to share with you because it has become very meaningful to me in my study of the *Tanakh*.

I had always looked at the *Tanakh* as Law (and history), as comprised of instruction, rules, and regulations for Israel to keep, and it does include all that. However, that is not the only theme of Moses and the Prophets in the *Tanakh*. Other themes run through the *Tanakh* that I had not clearly understood before. *HaShem* had the writers of Scripture, beginning with Moses, carry these themes throughout their books though they were separated by centuries. You all know that the Law is a theme but not the primary and only theme. Follow with me the themes that Moses began and the prophets enlarged upon:

- Seed Theme
- King Theme
- Prophet Theme
- Blessing Theme
- Faith Theme
- The Theme of the Covenants
- The Theme of G-d's working through Israel

- The Theme of the Nature and Essence of G-d.
- Law Theme

We will not now deal with all these themes that originated with Moses. Let us chart our way through the *Tanakh* and briefly look at one particular theme, the **Seed** that *HaShem* carried through His revelation to us. He placed all of these other themes in tandem with the **Seed** theme and the plurality of *Elokim* that has already been discussed.

The Seed Prophecy

Genesis 3:15

The first theme that arises from the writings of Moses is found in Genesis 3:15. This has to do with the promise that *HaShem* gave to Satan in the audience of Adam and Eve, and it is as follows:

> *And I will put enmity between you [Satan] and the woman, and between your seed and her seed; he shall bruise your head, and you shall bruise his heel.*
> [Harkavy Version]

Man had sinned against *HaShem* by eating of the only forbidden tree in the garden, *the tree of knowledge of good and evil* (Genesis 2:9). The Garden of Eden was full of fruit trees, and only one of them had a restriction on it. Eve was deceived; Adam ate knowingly of the fruit that Satan who indwelt the Serpent tempted them with. In Genesis 3 *HaShem Elokim* entered the scene; and after a discussion with Adam and Eve, *HaShem* made the first prophecy in the *Tanakh*, and it was addressed to Satan as we just read.

There are several points that need to be observed. Primarily there is going to be enmity between the **Seed** of the woman and the seed of the Satan. It is more than the enmity between woman and snakes. The **Seed** of the woman will crush the head of the serpent while the serpent will only be able to bruise the heel of the **Seed** of the woman. Two questions need to be asked:

1. First, does woman have seed?

The answer is, no. A woman has an egg which the male seed fertilizes, when those two things unite, an offspring (seed) is produced. In our case our seed/offspring is strictly human. Now we are also spirit beings, but we are confined to a human body, whereas spirit beings (angels/demons) are free to roam on earth as well as space of the universe. So how do we have an offspring/seed coming only from a woman? You say impossible! Humanly speaking you are 100 percent correct. So why does *HaShem* refer to the **Seed**/offspring of the woman implying that a man is not involved?

There is only one place in the *Tanakh* that the *seed of the woman* is referenced and it is here in Genesis 3:15 in *HaShem*'s first prophetic announcement. *HaShem* does not explain it here, not until Isaiah the Prophet do you get an explanation. Everywhere else in the *Tanakh* seed is always reckoned from the man who had sexual intercourse with a woman who then would give birth. Throughout the biblical text, Jewish tribal identity was always through the man, not the woman. So why is *HaShem* using the term *seed* (offspring) *of the woman*? Because G-d will energize the egg of a woman through His Word so that she will be able to give birth without the involvement of a man, in others words a virgin will conceive and give birth. It will be a supernatural act of G-d, a miracle.

2. The second question is: Can a human being touch Satan to destroy him or crush him?

The answer is an emphatic NO. First let us identify who Satan is: according to Isaiah 14:12-14 and Ezekiel 28:11-19 Satan was a created being, a spirit being, whose position was the *anointed cherub* that covered the throne of *HaShem* (Isaiah 14:12-14; Ezekiel 28:13-15) before *iniquity was found* in him. He was the highest order of angels and his position was as the covering, the *hupah* over the throne of *HaShem*. Satan, originally known as Lucifer, when he fell or iniquity was found in him became a very powerful adversary of *HaShem*. His objective was to be like the Most High, he wanted to be equal to *Elokim*. So in the heavens of *Elokim* he is in open rebellion against his creator. So from our perspective as humans, he is powerful and he is no pushover.

G-d remains in control and Satan is limited to his activities by the will of *Elokim* (Job 1:8-12; 2:4-7). Satan is a created being who rebelled and is the source of all the worship of manmade gods, anti-Semitism and sin. Despite Satan's attempt to be equal to G-d, the G-d of Abraham, Isaac and Jacob is G-d alone and there is no other G-d (Isaiah 43:10-11; 44:6; 45:5-6). There are NOT two G-ds dueling it out for supremacy.

Now back to our original question, can a human being touch Satan? The answer is no, because he is a powerful spirit foe and we are no match for him. Now back to the original statement of the Seed of the woman crushing Satan. The **Seed** of the woman will be more than human, he will be *Elokim*, but in flesh. This supernatural birth, will produce a birth of One who will crush Satan and remove the curse of sin on mankind and on the earth, however *HaShem* does not explain it for 3,000 years until His prophetic passage in Isaiah 7:14.

Now in the pre-flood world let's look at how Eve, Lamech and Satan himself understood the promise of the **Seed** of the Woman.

Genesis 4:1

How did Eve understand the prophecy from *HaShem Elokim*? We find the answer in Genesis 4:1 when she gives birth to her firstborn son:

> *And Adam knew Eve his wife; and she conceived, and bore Cain, and said, I have gotten a man from the LORD.*

All translations, both Jewish and Christian, add the phrase "from the" or "from the help of" the *L-RD*. However, in the Hebrew it simply says, *I have gotten a man, the LORD.* When she conceived and bore Cain, Eve understood part of *HaShem Elokim*'s prophecy. She said *I have gotten a man, the LORD.* What she said was I have given birth to a man who is the *L-RD*, the G-d/man who was to redeem them from the curse of sin. That was her understanding according to the text. However, it probably did not take her long to see that Cain was not that **Seed**; yet the promise still remained.

Genesis 5:28-29

The Promise of the **Seed** was well known in the pre-flood world. Lamech also understood the promise when he named Noah. Now Noah was not that **Seed**, but look what Lamech understood concerning the curse and the removal of it (Genesis 3:17-19) and the connection to the **Seed**:

> *This same* [Noah] *shall comfort us concerning our work and toil of our hands, because of the ground which the LORD hath cursed.*

We see how Eve and Lamech understood the Seed. The woman's perspective was with childbirth, whereas the man's perspective had to do with the curse on the earth.

Genesis 6:1-5

The next observation is how Satan understood *HaShem Elokim*'s prophecy about his own destruction. In Genesis 6, Satan responds to *HaShem Elokim*'s prophecy concerning the **Seed** of the woman. Satan sought to corrupt the **Seed** of the woman before he, the anticipated redeemer and comforter, could be born, thus preventing his birth. Eve at first saw this as being fulfilled in her firstborn son but was mistaken. Lamech believed the promise would be fulfilled through Noah. Of course the promise would eventually be fulfilled by a future redeemer and savior in the seed line. Satan understood he needed to corrupt the Seed promise of Genesis 3:15 that would bring forth this redeemer and comforter.

> *[1] And it came to pass, when men began to multiply on the face of the earth, and daughters where born unto them, [2] That the* **sons of God** *saw the daughters of men that they were fair; and they took them for wives of all whom they chose. [3] And the LORD said, My spirit shall not strive with man for ever, for that he is but flesh, and his days shall be a 120 years. [4] There were* **giants in the earth** *in those days; and also after that, when the sons of God came in unto the daughters of men, and they bore children to them, that same became mighty men who were of old, men of renown. [5] And God saw that the wickedness of man was great in the earth, and that every imagination of the thoughts of his heart was only evil continually.*

Here we have the background information for the purpose of the deluge, the worldwide flood to destroy man from off the earth except for Noah and his family, who alone were righteous in that day. Much can be said about this passage but there are two things that need to be defined and discussed. Who are the *sons of God* mentioned in the text? Who and what were the *giants in the earth*? We do see clearly that the imagination *of the thoughts of the heart* of man was *evil continually*. Notice as well *HaShem* does not leave the door open for the rabbinic teaching of a good and evil inclination. *HaShem* said that the thoughts of the heart (singular, not plural), were bent on the evil continually. In verse 4 the product of the *sons of G-d* with the *daughters of men* were *giants*. The term *sons of God* is used in the Hebrew Scriptures always for the angels of G-d and not the supposed righteous line of Seth, the third son of Adam. Some try to make Genesis 6 the exception to all the other passages, but there is nothing to warrant this exception.

Let us review the background of the word *giant* in connection to the *sons of God*. In Hebrew the word is *Nephilim*, meaning "fallen ones," but who are they? Here the Septuagint (LXX) gives us some very valuable information as to their identity. All of the *Tanakh* was translated in Greek long before the time of *Yeshua* [Jesus]. The LXX is the Greek translation of the Hebrew *Tanakh* done by seventy rabbis who responded to the call by Ptolemy Philadelphus (285-246 BCE) to do the translation of the Books of Moses [*Torah*] into Greek. These translators went to Alexandria, Egypt around 250 BCE to complete this task. So in 250 BCE how did the rabbis of that day understand Genesis 6:4 and the *Nephilim*? They translated the word *Nephilim* into the Greek word *gigentes*. Later it was transliterated, not translated, into English as *giants*. But

83

giant is not the meaning of the Greek word *gigentes*. These were the *Titans* in Roman/Greek mythology.

Those rabbis doing the Greek translation of the *Tanakh* understood *Titans* as a union not of two types of human beings, but of fallen angels (demons) and human women, and that such a union produced a being that was neither angelic nor human. They produced a new race of beings[32] call *Nephilim*, or fallen ones. The Greek/Roman mythologies were as follows: These *gigentes* were superhuman, but not in size. These Roman/Greek mythologies record how the gods from Mount Olympus had sexual union with humans on earth and produced children who had superhuman characteristics. This was Satan's strategy to destroy the **Seed** promised by *HaShem Elokim* in Genesis 3:15. He was on track to do so, so *Elokim* destroyed the world by water and imprisoned those demons[33] and then started over with Noah and his family. This is how Satan understood *HaShem Elokim*'s prophecy in Genesis 3:15 and how he responded to it.

The point that we need to grasp is that mankind is caught in the middle of a heavenly conflict between Satan, formerly an *anointed cherub* who now continues in open rebellion against his Creator. Satan is the god of this world and current world system and is in open warfare with *HaShem* the Creator. You as Jewish people are the epicenter of that

---

[32] Just to clarify a commonly misused word: race; there is only one race, the human race. However, in the human race there are many nationalities and ethnicities that make up all the families of the earth. There is no Black race, Asian race, European race, Spanish race or Jewish race. We are all members of the human race.

[33] See the New Testament Epistles of Peter and Jude: 2 Peter 2:4-5; Jude 6-7.

conflict. This ongoing conflict is the underlying impetus for worldwide anti-Semitism today. Satan does not want G-d's promised redeemer to succeed as the rightful Prince of Peace promised in Isaiah 9:6 [5]. Although Satan will ultimately fail, he will continue to do everything he can to prevent the Messiah from ending his rule on earth. Messiah's heel will crush Satan's head, as Genesis 3:15 prophesies.

Genesis 22:18

The **Seed** shows up next with the call of Abraham in Genesis 12:1-3, 7. In the Abrahamic Covenant, *HaShem* promised Abraham that he would have seed forever, and you, the Jewish people of today, are part of that fulfillment. However, in Genesis 14, Abraham's big concern was having no seed at all. In Genesis 21:1-3 Abraham received the promise of a seed and that seed line through Isaac was confirmed in Genesis 21:12. Then in Genesis 22:18, roughly 25 years after the birth of Isaac, Abraham was promised a **Seed** and that was well after the birth of Isaac. Now seed in the *Tanakh* is always singular, either as an absolute seed or plural seed. Abraham is promised that his seed will be as the stars of heaven and the sand on the seashore, and that is plural yet singular seed. But in Genesis 22:18 the promise of the **Seed** is an absolute singular referring to the **Seed** that *HaShem Elokim* prophesied in Genesis 3:15.[34] Even back in ancient history the patriarchs were looking for the promised **Seed**, who would be the Messiah in their future.

---

[34] See New Testament book of Galatians 3:16, 19.

The Seed Will Yield a King from Judah

Genesis 49:9-10

Next the promised **Seed** would be identified by Jacob in Genesis 49:9-10 as a **King** coming from the tribe of Judah:

> [9] *Judah is a lion's whelp: from the prey, my son, thou art gone up: he stooped down, he* **couched as a lion**, *and as an old lion; who shall rouse him up?* [10] *The sceptre shall not depart from* **Judah**, *nor a lawgiver from between his feet,* **until he come to Shiloh**; *and* **unto him shall the gathering of the peoples be**.

From this passage we understand that the **Seed** will come through the tribe of Judah. Jacob is also making three general statements as to the coming **Seed**.

- First of all the sceptre, the **kingship** of this **Seed,** will come from the tribe of Judah. This is an interesting prophecy by Jacob, because Judah will have to have leadership authority when the **King** comes.

- Secondly, Judah will have to have its identity intact as a tribe. There was a point in Jewish history when all the genealogical records of the tribes of Israel, including Judah, were lost—actually destroyed—in 70 CE when the Romans destroyed the temple. From that point on in Israel's history up to today, no Jewish person can identify his tribe with the exception of the tribe of Levi. But even they do not have an actual genealogy. Tribal identity and most importantly the identity of Judah is lost, meaning that the Messiah the **King** would have to come while Judah still had governmental leadership and the genealogy of Judah was still intact. That meant that it had to happen before the destruction of the city and the sanctuary [temple].

- Thirdly, the phrase *Until Shiloh comes* or *until he come to Shiloh* is not in the older texts of the *Tanakh*. *Shiloh* is used to distract from the real meaning. First the word *Shiloh* is not a proper name but a place where the Tabernacle first stood in the Land. Rabbis connect *Shiloh* to *Shilyah* which is the amniotic sac in the womb where the fetus is formed. Rabbis associate the two words to show that Messiah will be born of a woman, thus not divine. However, Genesis 3:15 is clear that the **Seed** of the woman comes from a woman and not by a sexual union of man and woman; it speaks of something supernatural happening though not explained. Moses in Genesis 3 clearly spoke to that point using Genesis 4 with Eve's understanding, Genesis 5 with Lamech's understanding and Genesis 6 with Satan's action or response against the **Seed** to be born. Also the Septuagint, Dead Sea Scrolls and the Syriac Version (Peshitta), which are all much older than the Masoretic Text by nearly a 1000 years or more do not use the word *Shiloh*. The phrase has a close association with Ezekiel 21:27, and the phrase from Genesis 49:10 should be rendered *until he comes to whom it belongs*. Let me quote two versions much older than the Masoretic Text:

> *A ruler shall not fail from Judah, nor a prince from his loins, until there come the things stored up for him; and he is the expectation of nations.* (Septuagint LXX)

> *The sceptre shall not depart from Judah, nor a lawgiver from between his feet, until the coming of the One to whom the sceptre*

belongs, to whom the Gentiles shall look forward. (Peshitta, Syriac Version)

This means that when the **Seed** comes to whom the sceptre belongs, it is to the **King**, the Messiah, that the people are to gather. That means Moses wrote that **King** Messiah would have to come before Judah would lose its tribal identity. That identity loss occurred in 70 CE when the Romans destroyed *the city and the sanctuary* (Daniel 9:27) and all genealogical records were destroyed.

I do not want you to miss the theme of **Faith** as we deal with the **Seed** and **King** themes. **Faith** or believing in the words of *Elokim* causes us to walk in His ways. See how the main characters of the Books of Moses are men of **Faith**:

- Abel lived by **Faith**—Genesis 4

- Enoch walked by **Faith** in *Elokim*—Genesis 5

- Noah lived by **Faith** and was righteous in his generation—Genesis 6-9

- Abraham lived by **Faith** and was called by *Elokim* His friend (2 Chronicles 20:7; Isaiah 41:8) and righteous—Genesis 15:6.

- Isaac walked by **Faith**—Genesis 21-27, 35

- Jacob walked by **Faith** with the exception of deceiving his father Isaac—Genesis 25-49

- Joseph lived by **Faith** and *Elokim* used him to provide safety and security for his father and his brothers and families—Genesis 37-50

- Moses, who walked by **Faith** and had a unique relationship with *HaShem*, was known as the man who knew G-d face to face (Deuteronomy 34:10).

- Israel was tested by *HaShem* to see if she would walk in **Faith** before Him. Sometimes they did, but many times they did not believe and trust in *HaShem* of which two incidents stand out. One of them was the golden calf worship while Moses was on Mt. Sinai receiving the Law and the pattern to build the Tabernacle (Exodus 32:1-10). The other big area of unbelief was Israel's rebellion against going into the land because of the majority report of the spies sent to Canaan (Numbers 14:1-12). *HaShem* said to Moses in Numbers 14:11 which illustrates the theme of **Faith** with these words:

> *How long will this people provoke me? And how long will it be that they believe me, for all the signs which I have shown among them.*

The theme of **Faith** stands out as a very predominate theme in the Books of Moses, and that **Faith** theme continues with Joshua, Boaz and Ruth, Samuel, David, Nathan, Elijah, Elisha and many more throughout the Writings and the books of the Prophets.[35]

Numbers 24:9, 17

The next major prophecy of the **Seed** relating to the **King** is recorded in Numbers 24:9, 17 where *HaShem* takes over the mouth of Balaam in his attempt to curse Israel. He ends up blessing Israel much to his and the King of Moab's dismay. Here are two of those verses out of a lengthy portion of the oracles of Balaam which speak of the **Seed** and **King**:

> [9] *He couched, he lay down as a lion and as a great lion: who shall stir him up? Blessed is he that blesses you, and cursed is he that curses you.*

---

[35] See the New Testament Epistle to the Hebrews, chapter 11.

[17] *I shall see him, but not now: I shall behold him,*
but not nigh: there shall come a **Star** *out of Jacob,*
and a **Sceptre** *shall rise out of Israel, and shall*
smite the corners of Moab, and destroy all the
children of Sheth.

What *HaShem* does through the mouth of Balaam is
prophesy of the **King** and connects him with Jacob's
blessing of Judah in Genesis 49:9 by using the phrase
concerning the couching lion:

[9] Judah is a lion's whelp: from the prey, my son,
thou art gone up: he stooped down, he **couched as**
a lion, *and as an old lion; who shall rouse him up?*

But *HaShem*, also through the mouth of Balaam, connects
the **Seed** and the **King** to the Abrahamic Covenant in
Genesis 12:3 which says: *And I will bless them that bless*
you, and curse him that curses you. Then he stated again
that out of Jacob would come a *Star*, a *scepter* in verse 17.[36]
The continued promise is recorded in the Books of Moses,
the *Torah* concerning the **Seed** and **King**. The singular **Seed**
was longed for by the Nation of Israel even in the time of
Moses during the exodus from Egypt.

The Seed King Will Be a Prophet

Deuteronomy 18:15-19

The last passage comes from Moses in Deuteronomy
18:15-19 where he continues to clarify the **Seed** and the
King with the word **Prophet**. Moses wrote:

---

[36] See the Gospel of Matthew in the New Testament in 2:1-12.

15 The **LORD** your God will raise up unto you a **Prophet from the midst of you**, *of your brethren,* **like unto me;** *unto him you shall hearken;* *16* *According to all that you desired of the LORD your God in Horeb in that day of the assembly, saying, Let me not hear again the voice of the LORD my God, neither let me see this great fire any more, that I die not.* *17* *And the* **LORD** **said unto me**, *they have well spoken that which they have spoken.* *18* **I will raise them up a Prophet** *from among your brethren,* **like unto you,** *and will* **put my words in his mouth;** *and* **he shall speak unto them all that I shall command him.** *19* *And it shall come to pass, that whosoever will not hearken unto my words which* **he shall speak in my name,** *I will require it of him.*

In this passage Moses is giving Israel guidance on how to discern a false prophet from a true prophet (verses 20-22). In verse 15 Moses tells the people that in the future *HaShem* will raise up a **Prophet** like unto himself. Then *HaShem* in verses 18 through 19 adds to that by saying several more things about this **Prophet**. The question that needs to be asked is, "How will this **Prophet** be *like Moses*?" One thing is obvious; He will speak the very words of G-d as Moses did. The rabbis have said many things about this subject, but they have missed the point. How will this future Prophet be like Moses?

Numbers 12:5-8

The answer to how the **Prophet** will be *like Moses* leads us to the next passage in Numbers 12:5-8. Here we have a passage concerning sibling rivalry between Aaron and Miriam against Moses:

91

⁵ And the LORD came down in the pillar of the cloud, and stood in the door of the tabernacle, and called Aaron and Miriam: and they both came forth. ⁶ And he said, hear now my words: If there be a prophet among you, I the LORD will make myself known unto him in a **vision** *and will speak unto him in a* **dream**. *⁷* **My servant Moses is not so**, *who is faithful in all mine house. ⁸ With him will I speak* **mouth to mouth**, *even apparently, and not in dark speeches; and* **the similitude of the *LORD* shall he behold**: *wherefore then were you not afraid to speak against my servant Moses?*

In this statement *HaShem*, the *Shechinah* presence of *Elokim*, announced to Aaron and Miriam two very important things that show Moses' uniqueness, foreshadowing what this future **Prophet** would be like. In verse 8 *HaShem* states that (1) with Moses He spoke *mouth to mouth* or **face to face**, and (2) that Moses **beheld the very form of *HaShem***. This is the uniqueness of Moses. No other prophet could add that to his resume—not Samuel, Elijah, Isaiah, Jeremiah, Daniel or Zechariah. As great as they were they never could claim those two unique characteristics of Moses as they belonged to Moses alone.

The **Prophet** of Deuteronomy 18:18-19 will talk with *HaShem* face to face, and He also will behold the very form of *HaShem*. So who will He be?[37] There is a clue in Deuteronomy 18:16-17 (quoted on page 90). Here *HaShem* their *Elokim* states to Moses that it was good for them to ask for a less terrifying approach to G-d, for G-d would speak to Israel in the future through His **Prophet**. The uniqueness of

---

[37] See the New Testament Gospel of John 1:18; 5:37, 39, 46; 6:46; 10:30-38; 14:8-9.

that **Prophet** stands out as the one who would come in the flesh as G-d Himself and speak directly to Israel in the voice of a man and not as the *Shechinah* from Mt. Sinai, an encounter that terrified the people. The point that should not be missed is that the Prophet will speak *face to face* with *HaShem*, and secondly this Prophet will also *behold the very form of HaShem*.

So Moses spoke of the **Seed** as a supernatural birth from Genesis 3:15 (as we will discuss later in connection with Isaiah 7:14), the **King** that has to come while Judah still has its tribal identity, and the **Prophet** like Moses who will speak directly with *HaShem* face to face and even behold His form. That is a very important and significant point to ponder, as Moses moves from the **Seed**, to the **King**, to the **Prophet** as he holds forth the deity of that coming Seed. In fact it is the very point that the prophets after Moses focus on—the deity and humanity of the **Prophet**, and they amplify what Moses said.

Deuteronomy 34:9-12

We want to observe one last passage in the Books of Moses before moving on to the Prophets and Writings sections of the Hebrew Scriptures.

What we find at the end of Deuteronomy is that the last two chapters of the book are not written by Moses but were added as an appendix by some other author. We first see that change in Deuteronomy 33:4 where it states the following: *Moses commanded us a law*.... Notice the change in pronouns to someone else. We do not know who that person was, but we do have a possible candidate. In Deuteronomy 34:9-12 we have the following statement:

⁹ And Joshua the son of Nun was full of the spirit of wisdom; for Moses had laid his hands upon him: and the children of Israel hearkened unto him and did as the LORD commanded Moses. **¹⁰ And there arose not a prophet since in Israel like unto Moses, whom the *LORD* knew face to face,** *¹¹ In all the signs and the wonders, which the LORD sent him to do in the land of Egypt to Pharaoh, and to all his servants, and to all his land, ¹² And in all that mighty hand, and in all the great terror which Moses shewed* [showed] *in the sight of all Israel.*

Verse 10 emphasizes there has not arisen *a prophet since in Israel like unto Moses, whom the LORD knew face to face.* Notice that the author confirms the uniqueness that *HaShem* said was Moses' and that no other prophet would have, until the **Prophet** to come who will be *like Moses.*

Years ago I was taught that the author of this section was probably Joshua, but the more I study the text I've come to the conclusion that it had to be someone else. You may ask, "Why?" My reasoning is that because Joshua is the immediate successor of Moses, there is no lapse of time between Moses and Joshua for verse 10 to have any meaning or connection whatsoever. This addition only makes sense if someone, for instance Ezra hundreds of years later in the 6th to 5th century BCE, looked back through Israel's history from Moses to himself to say, *there arose not a prophet since in Israel like unto Moses, whom the LORD knew face to face.* That makes complete textual sense.

So the *Torah*, the Five Books of Moses ends with a statement that the **Seed, King, Prophet,** whom we can now logically understand to be the Messiah, had not at that point in history come. His future appearance was yet to be. What we will see in the upcoming passages is that the Prophets will expand on the themes of Moses that will come through the Word of *HaShem* even more precisely as to the character, nature and timing of the long-awaited **Seed**, **King**, and **Prophet**, the Messiah of Israel.

Chapter Eight:
Messiah: Seed, King and Prophet in the Prophets

As we look into the Prophets and the Writings, each of these two divisions are connected to the Written Law of Moses because they are referring back to the commands that *HaShem* gave through Moses to Israel. The internal part was the living out of the commands of *HaShem* daily by **Faith** from the heart (Deuteronomy 6:5). The fruit of that would overflow externally in living out their **Faith** by works in their daily lives by being obedient to the 613 Laws of Moses. The theme of **Faith** is predominant with Moses, and it will continue through into the life of Joshua and other men like Samuel, David, Elijah and Daniel to name only a few. Joshua had already demonstrated faithfulness to the *L-RD* throughout his life but especially at Kadesh-barnea (Numbers 13:30; 14:6-9). He would again demonstrate his **Faith** by following the instructions of the Captain of the *L-RD*'s host when the walls of Jericho fell down flat in Joshua 6. Here is the connection or hinge between the Law and the Prophets section of the *Tanakh*:

> *This book of the law shall not depart out of thy mouth;* **but you shall meditate therein day and night,** *that you may* **observe to do according to all that is written therein;** *for* **then** *thou shall make*

your way prosperous, and then thou shall have good
success. (Joshua 1:8)

The Prophet division of your *Tanakh* begins with the fact that the law is not to depart or leave your mouth mechanically as a rote artificial act, but that His Word would saturate your heart. In this way, you are to meditate on the Written Law and observe it followed by assured prosperity and success. What a wonderful promise.

There are two different laws that you are aware of, the Written Law from Moses and what the rabbis claim as the Oral Law from Moses. However, there is no evidence from the Books of Moses [*Torah*] or from the Prophets and Writings sections that there ever was such a law. This Oral Law is a creation of the rabbis from the second temple period (450 BCE—70 CE), not from Moses.

Now back to Joshua. Look at the end of Joshua's life in Joshua 24 as he reviews all that *HaShem* has done for Israel and then tells them to choose between all the defeated gods and serve the living G-d of Israel. Notice at the end of verse 15 Joshua says, *but as for me and my house, we will serve the LORD*. Look as well at Israel's response to Joshua in verse 24:

And the people said unto Joshua, the LORD our God will we serve, and his voice will we obey.

Israel committed themselves the second time to the words of Joshua and to *HaShem*, to keep His law, but what happened? After Joshua and the elders who outlived Joshua all died, Israel largely had not had *HaShem*'s blessing because they did not keep His law. Israel did not meditate on the Written Law of *HaShem* nor did they observe the *Sh'ma*, especially verse 5. If verse 5 is not obeyed, the rest of the *Sh'ma* is just mechanical, artificial religious acts from *HaShem*'s perspective.

When we finish reviewing the Prophets we will look at the Writings, and we will see the same connection to meditate on the Word of *HaShem*. Living out G-D's law obediently comes from the heart, which is essential to having *HaShem's* blessing. Return in your thoughts to the theme of the **Seed**, **King** and **Prophet** concerning the coming son of David, the Messiah or *Moshiach*. The absolute singular aspect of the **Seed** in the Prophets becomes even more focused on the one person who will come, who is uniquely the **King** and **Prophet**. Our next passage narrows down again the focus of *Elokim* as to who this **Seed**, **King**, and **Prophet** is who will come.

2 Samuel 7 and 1 Chronicles 17

This next passage is quoted in both the Prophets and Writings divisions of the *Tanakh*. We will compare these two passages from 2 Samuel 7:11b-17 and 1 Chronicles 17:10b-15:

> *11b ... Also the LORD tells you that he will make you a house. 12 And when your* [David's] *days be fulfilled, and you shall sleep with your fathers, I will set up* **your seed** *after you, which shall* **proceed out of thy bowels** *and I will establish his kingdom. 13 He shall build an house for my name, and* **I will establish the throne of his kingdom for ever.** *14 I will be his father, and he shall be my son.* **If he commit iniquity,** *I will chasten him with the rod of men, and with the stripes of the children of men; 15 But my mercy shall not depart away from him* **as I took it from Saul,** *whom I put away before you. 16 And your house and* **your kingdom** *shall be*

established for ever before you: your throne shall be established for ever. ¹⁷ *According to all the words, and according to all this vision, so did Nathan speak unto David.*
(2 Samuel 7:11b-17)

^{10b} *Furthermore I tell you that the LORD will build you an* [a] *house* [or Dynasty]. ¹¹ *And it shall come to pass, when your days be expired that you must go to be with your fathers, that* **I will raise up your seed after you** [David], *which shall be* **of your sons;** *and* **I will establish his kingdom.** ¹² *He shall build me an* [a] *house and* **I will establish his throne for ever.** ¹³ *I will be his father, and he shall be my son; and I will not take my mercy away from him as I took it from him that was before you.* ¹⁴ **But I will settle him in mine house and in my kingdom for ever:** *and* **his throne shall be established for evermore.** ¹⁵ *According to all these words, and according to all this vision, so did Nathan speak unto David. (1 Chronicles 17:10b-15)*

Here through the mouth of Nathan the prophet we have recorded the words of *HaShem* concerning the Davidic Covenant wherein *Elokim* promises that David will never lack a man, a descendent to sit on David's throne (Jeremiah 33:17).

Notice the parts that are parallel and the parts that are different in both passages between 2 Samuel 7 and 1 Chronicles 17. Notice the parallel parts:

1. I will build David a house or dynasty;

2. His Kingdom and throne will be established forever;

3. *HaShem* will be his father;

4. He will be *HaShem's* son;

5. *HaShem*'s mercy will not be removed from Him;

6. He shall build Me a house.

Now notice the differences and similarities between the two passages, 2 Samuel 7 versus 1 Chronicles 17:

1. He will proceed from David directly in Samuel, but will proceed from David's sons in Chronicles;

2. Sin is mentioned—No sin mentioned;

3. He will settle him in my house and Kingdom forever;

4. He is an eternal son because his house, throne and Kingdom will be established forever in My house.

These two passages on the Davidic Covenant spoke of two persons coming from David. The Samuel passage views King Solomon, who came directly from David. Even though Solomon sinned against *HaShem*, the *L-RD* did not depart from him as He did from King Saul. Solomon built the temple in Jerusalem.

The second passage from Chronicles has the Messiah in view because He would come from the **sons** of David sometime beyond the life of David, and this one will not sin as Solomon did. He will be settled in *HaShem's* house, showing the eternality of this son. It is this son of David that will build the Millennial Temple (Zechariah 6:12-13) in Jerusalem in the future. We read in the Gospels of Matthew and Luke in the New Testament[38] that Joseph, the earthly step-father of *Yeshua*, was a descendent of Solomon; and Mary's [Miriam's] father, Heli, was a descendent of David through another of David's **sons**, Nathan. Notice that from Chronicles we see the Messiah did not have to come through Solomon but one of the other **sons** of David.

Also notice a point that will be developed by David in the Psalms, in Proverbs and Isaiah: *Elokim* will be His Father; this Messiah will be *HaShem*'s Son. We will see this as we come to them in the following passages in the *Tanakh*.

The Prophet Isaiah

The prophets mentioned in Samuel and Kings are called the former prophets. They were not writing prophets, so with the exception of Nathan the prophet they have little to say about the **Seed**, **King**, and **Prophet** who would be the Messiah of Israel. The former prophets were dealing with the kings of Judah: Saul, David and Solomon. After the kingdom split, the prophets Elijah and Elisha were dealing with Israel (the 10 northern tribes) and Judah (the two southern tribes of Judah and Benjamin). After the division, Israel in the north had no king who obeyed *HaShem*'s commands and walked after Him. The first king, Jeroboam of the northern tribes, set up a corrupted form of the worship of *HaShem*. It was the same sin that angered *HaShem* in the wilderness, the worship of the golden calf. Compare 1 Kings 12:25-33 with Exodus 32:7-35.

Jeroboam in 1 Kings 12:28 quoted exactly what Aaron did when he made the golden calf in Exodus 32:4: *These be thy gods, O Israel, which brought you up out of the land of*

---

[38] See the New Testament Gospels of Matthew and Luke: Matthew 1:1:17 and Luke 3:23-38.

Egypt. However, Judah had some good kings and some bad kings, so the early prophets like Elijah and Elisha recorded in those books spoke to the apostasy of Israel and warned Judah not to follow Israel in its apostasy. But Judah did not listen. Even though they had some good kings, their repentance was never at the level before their apostasy. There was a circular downward cycle.

Isaiah the prophet was a writing prophet, and his ministry was contemporary with King Ahaz, a very wicked king, and King Hezekiah, a very good king in Judah. Isaiah saw the handwriting on the wall and understood that Judah was sliding into the sin and apostasy that destroyed Israel in the north. So he has much to say about judgment as well as hope. I want to reference the first five chapters of Isaiah because rabbinic Judaism teaches that sin is not inherited in every human being from Adam's sin. There is something called the sin nature, meaning that sin is imputed to every descendent of Adam and Eve because of the sin in the Garden of Eden. Yet Jewish people have been given rabbinic inventions called *the inclination of good* (*yetzer ha-tov*) and the *inclination for evil* (*yetzer ha-ra*) to avoid the concern of an imputed sin nature. However, the Hebrew Scriptures are abundant with verses and examples of the depravity of Israel and Judah, and man's sinful heart which is laid out clearly in the first five chapters of Isaiah as well as Isaiah 59:1-15 as he speaks of Israel (Judah). Because of sin our good works merit nothing before a holy G-d in fact *HaShem* considers all of man's good works as filthy rags (unclean menstrual cloths) in Isaiah 64:6.

In Isaiah chapters 1-5 *HaShem* lays out a scathing report and indictment on Judah; it is not a pretty picture. If you have a *Tanakh* in your home, pick it up and go to Isaiah and read the first five chapters. It will begin to set the stage for the writing prophets that we will be visiting.

Isaiah 7-12 – The Book of Immanuel

Of the next six passages in Isaiah three of them will come out of the Book of Isaiah, chapters 7 through 12, which together are called the Book of Immanuel; the other three passages will come from Isaiah 49, 50 and 53. *Immanuel* means *G-d with us*.[39]

Birth of Messiah - Isaiah 7:14

The first passage comes from Isaiah 7, but before the verses are quoted a very brief reflection is needed on what Isaiah 7:13-14 is all about. If you have a *Tanakh* in your home, start at verse 1 and read up through verse 16.

Isaiah is instructed by *HaShem* to go and meet wicked King Ahaz of Judah, and Isaiah is to take his son Shear-jashub with him (vs. 3). His son's name means "a remnant shall return." Ahaz was very worried for he knew that Syria and Israel were plotting to attack Jerusalem, depose him and replace him with someone who was not from the house of David. Syria and Israel wanted Judah to fight with them against the growing threat of Assyria, and King Ahaz would not cooperate with them. He was greatly concerned because he knew that he could not withstand an coordinated attack from both Syria and Israel, and he was out checking on his fortifications and water supply. *HaShem* then told King Ahaz through Isaiah that the coming threat would not succeed against him, and in fact his adversaries would be destroyed before they could accomplish what they desired. Now *HaShem* said through Isaiah that He would give King

---

[39] See the New Testament Gospel of Matthew 1:20-23.

Ahaz any sign that he wished to show him that the throne of David was secure. Ahaz declines the sign because he does not want to be responsible to *HaShem*. So *HaShem* through Isaiah gave him a sign anyway. Pay close attention to the singular and plural usages in the next six verses. In Isaiah 7:10-12 Isaiah spoke to King Ahaz in the **singular**, but then in verses 13 to 14 Isaiah spoke to the house of David in the **plural**, meaning to the whole house of David. Isaiah then in verses 15 to 16 returns to speaking to King Ahaz, using **singular** pronouns because once again *HaShem* was speaking through Isaiah to King Ahaz alone, and not to the house of David. Look at it in a simpler way:

- In verses 10-12, Isaiah used **singular pronouns** and spoke directly **to Ahaz**.

- In verses 13-14, Isaiah then switched to **plural pronouns** and spoke **to the house of David**.

- In verses 15-16, Isaiah then went back to **singular pronouns** because he was speaking again directly **to King Ahaz**.

Isaiah is speaking to two audiences. These pronouns have a significant role in the understanding of this passage. In verses 13-14, the passage of interest, *HaShem* did not speak just to King Ahaz but to the whole house of David, giving Ahaz and the tribe of Judah the following sign:

[13] And he said, Hear you now, O house of David; is it a small thing for you to weary men, but will you weary my God also?
[14] Therefore the Lord himself shall give you a sign: Behold, a young woman [virgin] *shall conceive, and bear a son, and shall call his name Immanuel.*

This sign was to the whole house of David of which King Ahaz was a part. This verse has brought about much controversy among rabbis and Jewish people over the centuries as well as among liberal unbelieving christians of the last 200 years. Let us look together at the italicized words from the text individually.

First, notice it is to the *house of David*. Second, you have the word *behold* in verse 14. This word is a Hebrew present participle showing an act of *HaShem* that is yet to come, and this is very important to grasp. Thirdly are the words *young woman* or *virgin*, which are at the core of this passage. The word is *almah* in the Hebrew, meaning a young woman who has never been married who is also a virgin. Rabbinic Judaism chaffs at this verse because New Testament believers use this verse to show that *Yeshua* [Jesus] was the Messiah of Israel born of a *virgin*, fulfilling the promise from Genesis 3:15. Rabbinic Judaism says that the Hebrew word *betulah*, not *almah*, is used to indicate the meaning of virgin; however that does not coincide with Joel 1:8 where a *betulah* is a widow who would hardly be a virgin. They argue further that *almah* is just a young woman, *but the term betulah* would be used to clarify a young woman who is a virgin. However this birth is to be a *sign* from G-d. A young woman getting pregnant is hardly a *sign* from G-d; it happens every day in every country, in every year and every decade of every century around the world. But a virgin getting pregnant is a *sign*, and it is completely unique. But still they put forth the idea that it was a young woman living then who would conceive and give birth to a son, and rabbis imply that this promised son is Hezekiah. Hezekiah, even though he was a good king, was not the Messiah promised by the Prophets, for he was a vassal king giving tribute to Assyria (Isaiah 36), not a fulfillment of the prophets. Nor was Hezekiah the Prophet *like unto Moses* as prescribed in Deuteronomy 18, which was looked at in chapter six of this book. The rabbinic view does not coincide with the whole of the *Tanakh*.

Let us look further; *Betulah* does not actually mean a virgin but instead it means a young woman in the Hebrew text, which is the opposite of what rabbinic Judaism says. Here are two reasons why the position of rabbinic Judaism cannot be true. First, as mentioned before in Joel 1:8 a *betulah* is a widow, and a woman cannot be a widow and be a virgin; marriage erases virginity. Also in Genesis 24:16 Rachel, the future wife of Isaac, was called a *betulah;* and then Moses further defines *betulah* by saying that she was an *almah*, a virgin (Genesis 24:43). *Almah* is used seven times in the *Tanakh*, and each one of them is referencing a virgin.

Fourthly, another important point that needs to be given is to show how the sages understood the verse long before *Yeshua* [Jesus] became an issue. What we will find is that rabbis from Rashi to the present day are in complete denial of what sages said before them and even before the Common Era as to what they taught and understood about the word *almah*. I referenced this earlier concerning the Septuagint which was translated from the Hebrew into Greek many years before the birth of *Yeshua* (Jesus). The Septuagint became the Bible for all Hellenized Jewish people outside of the land of Israel for centuries. How did the ancient sages understand the word *almah* in their day, and what Greek word did they use when they translated it to convey the meaning of *almah*? The Greek word that they used was *parthenos*, which clearly and without question means *virgin* in the Greek. So rabbinic Judaism of today either ignores the verse or changes its interpretation to avoid any possibility of pointing to *Yeshua* as the *virgin* born Messiah of Israel. This confusion of the meaning of words is not being honest with the text of *HaShem*'s Word or with the Jewish people.

Another argument from the rabbis is that if it were pointing to *Yeshua* [Jesus] who was born 700 years later, how would that be a comfort to Ahaz who had serious issues on his hands then, such as his personal survival and the survival of the Davidic dynasty? That is a valid question that needs to be answered. As stated six paragraphs earlier, the singular pronouns Isaiah used in reference to King Ahaz changed to plural pronouns that referenced the whole house of David in verses 13 to 14. *HaShem* was saying to the house of David that the kingship of David's dynasty must be intact when this virgin gives birth (Genesis 49:10), for it will be a supernatural birth, reflective of the promised **Seed** in Genesis 3:15.

Another point to consider is to remember *HaShem Elokim's* prophecy back in Genesis 3:15 of the **Seed** of the woman that would come and defeat Satan. Remember as well women do not have seed, so how can a virgin conceive? Humanly speaking it was impossible. Now can't *HaShem* who spoke the heavens and earth into existence by the breath of His mouth (Genesis 1; Psalm 33:6; Isaiah 43:15; 44:24; 48:12-13) also speak the word to have a virgin's egg fertilized to fulfill a prophecy He personally made over 3,000 years earlier? Would that not be a simple task for Him? *HaShem* is amplifying that original prophecy in Genesis 3:15 with more information, and now He is calling that one who would be born *Immanuel, G-d with us*. But that is still of no consequence to King Ahaz.

This prophecy does not have a double fulfillment. It is two different prophecies, not one as most view it, that were given to King Ahaz and to the house of David. It is two prophecies, one in the near future specifically for King Ahaz

108

(verses 15-16) and one in the distant future for the house of David (verses 13-14), signifying the virgin birth. In verse 3 *HaShem* told Isaiah to take his son with him. This needs to be remembered because the prophecy contains the timing that refers to the near future for King Ahaz. The pronouns once again shift back to the singular in verses 15-16. Isaiah likely is picking up his young son, probably a toddler in his arms, as he states these two verses:

> [15] *Butter and honey shall he eat, when he knows to refuse the evil, and choose the good.* [16] *For before* **the child** *shall know* **to refuse the evil and choose the good,** *the land that thou abhor shall be forsaken of both her kings.*

HaShem told Isaiah to take Shear-jashub his son with him so that Isaiah could use him as an object lesson to differentiate between the two prophecies and to comfort King Ahaz. King Ahaz's comfort is that when this child, Isaiah's son, when he knows the difference to refuse evil from good, the kings of Israel and Syria will no longer be a threat to him because Assyria will have already conquered them. So the threat personally to King Ahaz and collectively to the house of David is gone.

In summary, verses 13 to 14 are to be fulfilled in the distant future (700 years later) and verses 15 to 16 were fulfilled in the immediate future with the destruction of Israel (the ten northern tribes) and Syria. This answers all questions that refer to Ahaz's personal concerns as well as all the concerns of the House of David. This fits the context of Isaiah and explains the first prophecy given by *HaShem* Himself in Genesis 3:15. So there will be a supernatural birth initiated by *HaShem* Himself.

Before we move on to the next passage, what has *HaShem* said in the *Tanakh* about the *seed of the woman* up to this point in our study?

- Genesis 3:15—from a woman;

- Genesis 22:18—from a Jewish woman;

- Genesis 49:10—from a Jewish woman of the tribe of Judah who will give birth before Judah loses its tribal identity;

- 1 Chronicles 17—from a Jewish woman also from the line of David of the tribe of Judah;

- Isaiah 7:14—from a Jewish virgin—the miraculous way the **Seed** is conceived.

That is what *HaShem* has revealed in His Word to His people, the Jewish people. Now begin to weigh the evidence from Moses, Nathan and Isaiah. Moses presents the promised **Seed**, Jacob (Genesis 49:10) and Balaam (Numbers 24:9, 17) present the promised **Seed** as the **King**. Add together all the evidence as it begins to build that *Elokim* Himself will become flesh and dwell among His people as the **Prophet** *like unto Moses*. As we continue through the Prophets and Writings sections of the *Tanakh,* we see *HaShem* in His Word continuing to build this redemptive Messianic theme as He progressively reveals His Messiah to Israel.

Messiah—Human/Divine? Isaiah 9:6-7 [5-6]

The next passage also comes from the writings of Isaiah from the section called the "Book of Immanuel" which is found in Isaiah 9:6-7 [5-6]:

> [6] *For unto* **us a child is born***, unto us* **a son is given:** *and the government shall be upon his shoulder: and*

110

his name shall be called Wonderful Counselor, The mighty God, The everlasting Father, the Prince of Peace. ⁷ *Of the increase of* **his government and peace** *there shall be* **no end, upon the throne of David,** *and upon his kingdom to order it, and to establish it with judgment and with justice from hence forth* **even for ever.** *The zeal of the* **LORD of hosts will perform this.** (King James Version)

In these two verses we have another promise concerning the **Seed** who will be **King** and **Prophet**: the Messiah. This passage begins to focus on His character and person. First, to the Jewish people a child was to be born; He will be a human being. Second unto the Jewish people a son is given. Who is giving the son to the Jewish people? It is G-d who gives the son, His son, even as the prophet Nathan told David that the son from David's sons would be His son, as 1 Chronicles 17:13 states. Before we look at the descriptive names given this son, we need to understand that it isn't the Jewish people who name Him. *HaShem* names Him, which expresses His own leadership, Lordship and authority and confers it to the One who would be born, the Messiah. These are not names that belong to a person who is just a human being, but to *HaShem* Himself. However in the Jewish Bible words have been added to conceal the meaning of the text. What *HaShem* has done in His naming of the son whom He is giving may be shocking, but as we look at the descriptive names that *HaShem* gives to Him, the one to be born, we are led to some very clear conclusions as to His identity.

- *Wonderful Counselor*: The word *wonderful* is a Hebrew word "Pele" [פֶּלֶא or פֶּלֶא] that is only used of *HaShem* in the *Tanakh* (Genesis 18:14; Judges 13:18);

111

- *The mighty God*: or *El Gibbor*: This born one will be the mighty G-d to whom Israel will return (Isaiah 10:21).

- *The everlasting Father*: This title is referencing the Father of eternality, who is provider of eternal life. (Compare with Isaiah 63:16.)

- *The Prince of Peace:* All Jewish people believe that when Messiah comes He will bring Peace. The one ingredient of life that every Jewish person longs for is Peace.

Then as we continue to observe the text, this child who will be born, who has descriptive names that only *HaShem* would carry, will bear on his shoulders His government and peace that will have *no end*. The term *no end* is the strongest combination of words in the Hebrew language to speak of eternity and beyond time itself. Notice that His government will have *no end* upon the throne of David. Who will do this? *HaShem* Himself! Contrary to what the rabbis teach, the visible manifestation of *Elokim* will be born in human flesh as the **Seed** that will crush Satan. *HaShem* will become flesh. It is not as rabbinic Judaism says, a man becoming god, a mere man CANNOT become G-d, but it is G-d Himself taking on flesh to redeem us. He is to come to fulfill the Covenants to Abraham, David and to the nation of Israel and in the process will also deal with sin that has corrupted this earth. We will see more passages concerning the *son* when we get to the Writings section of the *Tanakh*.

Branch of Jesse – Isaiah 11:1-2

Once again in the Book of Immanuel, Isaiah lays out an unexpected aspect of the birth of the **Seed**, the Messiah. In Isaiah 11:1-2 states:

¹ And there shall come forth a rod out of the **stem** [stump] **of Jesse,** *and a* **Branch shall grow out of his roots:** *² And the* **spirit of the *LORD* shall rest upon him,** *the spirit of* **wisdom** *and* **understanding**, *the spirit of* **counsel** *and* **might**, *the spirit of* **knowledge** *and of the* **fear of the *LORD*.** [Brackets from the Jewish Study Bible – JPS].

It is not just that the spirit of the *L-RD* will be upon Him, because the spirit of the *L-RD* was upon men like Moses and David. However, this one will have the *fullness* of the Spirit, as described by six terms that reveal that His wisdom is not measured. When the Messiah comes, He will not come in royal pomp because He is of David, but He will come forth poor and insufficient as from Jesse, the father of David. He will come in insignificance, born in poverty! So the **Seed**, the **King**, the **Prophet** will be born in poverty; the Messiah's mother will be poor.[40]

Servant Who Redeems – Isaiah 49:1-6

The next verses are long, but I will observe with you a couple of points as we look at Isaiah 49:1-6. This whole section is very significant:

¹ Listen, O isles, unto me; and hearken, you people, from afar; The LORD has **called me from the womb; from the bowels of my mother** *hath he made mention of my name.*
² And he hath made my mouth like a sharp sword; in the shadow of his hand hath he hid me, and made me a polished shaft; in his quiver hath he hid me;

---

[40] Compare the New Testament Gospel of Luke 2:21-24 with Leviticus 12:8

³ And said unto me, **You are my servant, O Israel,** *in whom I will be glorified.*

⁴ Then I said, I have laboured in vain, I have spent my strength for nought, and in vain: yet surely my judgment is with the LORD, and my work with my God.

⁵ **And now, saith the *LORD* that formed me from the womb to be his servant,** *to* **bring Jacob again to him,** *That Israel be gathered unto him, and I was glorious in the eyes of the LORD, and my God shall be my strength.*

⁶ And he said, It is a light thing that you should be **my servant to raise up the tribes of Jacob, and to restore the preserved of Israel:** *I will also give you for a* **light to the nations** [Gentiles], *that thou mayest be* **my salvation unto the end of the earth.**

Notice in verses 1 and 5 that only the mother is mentioned. There is no mention of a father of the Messiah in any passage of the *Tanakh*. That would correspond with Genesis 3:15, the **Seed** of the woman. In verse 3 He is called by *HaShem my servant, O Israel*. Rabbinic Judaism wants to read the nation of Israel into this statement, but that presents problems. How in verse 5 can Israel [Jacob] bring itself [Israel] back to Him, when [Israel] itself is in need of salvation? This Servant will *bring Jacob again to him* [*HaShem*]. In verse 6 how can Israel raise up Israel? This reference again is pointing to the **Seed**, the **King**, the **Prophet**, the Servant who is the Messiah. Notice as well that he makes him a *light to the nations* [Gentiles]. He provides salvation, but what kind of salvation: physical or spiritual? The Gentiles as well as Israel have by practice since Genesis 3 condemned themselves to a life of separation from a Holy G-d because of their sin. The salvation here that

114

the Servant speaks of is spiritual salvation to restore the earth to its paradise condition before sin came into the world.

Who is the Servant? – Isaiah 53

Let me quote this passage in its entirety, starting in Isaiah 52:13 to 53:12. To forewarn you this passage does not come from the Christian Bible but from the Jewish Study Bible from the Jewish Publication Society. This passage comes from Isaiah 700 years before the destruction of the *city* and *sanctuary* in 70 CE. The rabbis skip over this passage in the synagogues and it is not reflected in the daily readings.

Isaiah 52:13 - 53:12

This passage of Scripture is astounding, but rabbinic Judaism has again placed an interpretation on it to point away from instead of to the Messiah. This redirection occurred with the great Jewish rabbi Rashi, who went against all the sages before him to give it a different interpretation. So why is his interpretation incorrect and misleading? First let us look at the passage in question:

52:13 Indeed, **My** *servant shall prosper, Be exalted and raised to great heights.*
52:14 Just as the many were appalled at **him,** *so marred was* **his** *appearance, unlike that of man,* **His** *form, beyond human semblance,*
52:15 Just so **he** *shall startle many nations. Kings shall be silenced because of* **him,** *for they shall see what has not been told them, shall behold what they never have heard.*
53:1 Who can believe what **we** *have heard? Upon whom has the arm of the LORD been revealed?*

^{53:2} *For* **he** *has grown, by* **His** *favor, like a tree crown, like a tree trunk out of arid ground.* **He** *had no form or beauty, that* **we** *should look at* **him:** *No charm, that* **we** *should find* **him** *pleasing.*

^{53:3} **He** *was despised, shunned by men, A man of suffering, familiar with disease. As one who* **hid** *his face from us,* **he** *was despised,* **we** *held* **him** *of no account.*

^{53:4} *Yet it was* **our** *sickness that* **he** *was bearing,* **Our** *suffering that* **he** *endured.* **We** *accounted* **him** *plagued, smitten and afflicted by God;*

^{53:5} *But* **he** *was wounded because of* **our** *sins, crushed because of* **our** *iniquities.* **He** *bore the chastisement that made* **us** *whole, and by* **his** *bruises* **we** *were healed.*

^{53:6} **We** *all went astray like sheep, each going his* **own** *way; and the LORD visited upon* **him** *the guilt of all of* **us.**

^{53:7} **He** *was maltreated, yet* **he** *was submissive,* **he** *did not open his mouth; Like a sheep being led to slaughter, like a ewe, dumb before those who shear her,* **he** *did not open his mouth.*

^{53:8} *By oppressive judgment* **he** *was taken away, who could describe* **his** *abode? For* **he** *was cut off from the land of the living through the sin of my people, who deserved the punishment.*

^{53:9} *And* **his** *grave was set among the wicked, and with the rich, in* **his** *death, though* **he** *had done no injustice and had spoken no falsehood.*

^{53:10} *But the LORD chose to crush* **him** *by disease, that if* **he** *made* **himself** *an offering for guilt,* **he** *might see offspring and have long life, and that* **through him** *the LORD's purpose might prosper.*

116

53:11 *Out of* **his** *anguish* **he** *shall see it;* **he** *shall enjoy it to the full through* **his** *devotion.* "**My** *righteous servant makes the many righteous, it is their punishment that* **he** *bears;*
53:12 *Assuredly, I will give* **him** *the many as* **his** *portion,* **he** *shall receive the multitude as* **his** *spoil. For* **he** *exposed* **himself** *to death and was numbered among the sinners, whereas* **he** *bore the guilt of the many and made intercession for sinners.* (Jewish Study Bible)

How has Rashi detracted from the true meaning of this passage? He applied the passage to Israel as being the Suffering Servant rather than applying it to the Messiah. There are several key points that need to be observed.

- All the sages before Rashi and even a few hundred years after Rashi with one voice declared that this passage referenced the Messiah, an Individual and not a collective group like the nation of Israel. So Rashi contradicts the sages, as well as the prophets like Isaiah, and *HaShem* Himself, the G-d of Israel. Back in chapter three we observed the statements of the sages as to anyone who would contradict them. Is the respected rabbi exempt from the words of the sages?

- Collective Israel does not fit the context. Look at the pronouns used: **we**, **us**, **our** and **he**, **him**, **his**. The *he*, *him* and *his* refers to an individual, and the *we*, *us*, and *our* refers to Isaiah and his people speaking in reaction to the Suffering Servant. Rashi once again reinterprets the usages of these pronouns to get away from the obvious.

- It's also commonly stated by Judaism that this passage described the sufferings of Israel at the hand of the Gentiles. However who is the writer of the

Book of Isaiah? Also, please notice his constant use of the pronouns *we*, *us* and *our* that speak of Isaiah's people. Notice as well that in verse 11 the Suffering Servant is called *my righteous servant* who will make many righteous. Isaiah presents Israel throughout his book as needing righteousness, not as the one who dispenses it.

• In verse 8 the term *cut off* means *death*, and the mention of the land of the living is a further contrast to being cut off. Rashi states that *cut off* means Israel being removed from the land of Israel. Once again Rashi has made an interpretation that is not in the text of *HaShem*'s Word.

• Also in verse 8 if Rashi's interpretation is taken literally, then when did Israel die? Never! Israel even in the Diaspora is referred to as a nation by Moses (Deuteronomy 30:1-6) and the Prophets (Ezekiel 37).

• In verses 4-7, when did Israel suffer voluntarily? Israel in all her suffering never suffered willingly, voluntarily or silently.

• In verses 10-12 when did Israel suffer vicariously for the Gentiles? The Scriptures state that Messiah will suffer for Israel and the Gentiles. How can a sinful nation like Israel (see again Isaiah chapters 1-5 and 59:1-15) suffer for another sinful people and justify both groups before G-d? It simply is not possible and shows a lack of knowledge of the holiness of *HaShem*.

• Also in verses 8-12 the Servant dies. Israel never died as a nation before G-d and never lost their nationhood before G-d. However, the Messiah dies. G-d's Messiah dies in His first coming and so does the false rabbinic messiah die, so this passage simply cannot be made to mean that Israel died.

118

- When was Israel resurrected from the dead? Israel never died to be resurrected. However, David (Psalm 16:10-11) and Isaiah (Isaiah 53:10, 12) spoke of Messiah's resurrection. Even the rabbinic messiah is taught to be resurrected.

- The Suffering Servant in verse 11 is called *my righteous servant*. One fact you know very well is that Israel was not righteous. If you doubt that, sit down, and read Isaiah, Jeremiah, Ezekiel, Hosea, Micah and the other prophets. Israel was many things but being righteous was not one of them. However, the Messiah that the Prophets spoke of was without sin, blameless and went to His death in silence so that He could out of love for His people be the voluntary, vicarious sacrifice for sins.

Read through this passage and challenge the status quo of Rashi's interpretation which rabbinic Judaism promotes today, and look at what *HaShem* said concerning the Suffering Servant, His *righteous servant*. Rashi knowingly opposed the sages who held the Suffering Servant as the Messiah for century after century after century. Why is this passage not read or discussed in synagogue readings on the Sabbath?

The Prophets Jeremiah

Isaiah has so much more to say, but let us move on to the prophet Jeremiah. We will observe two passages in the writings of Jeremiah.

Jeremiah 4:1-4

This reference seems to be an unlikely candidate to show the theme of the **Seed**, **King**, **Prophet** and **Blessing** that the Messiah will bring to Israel and to the world. This passage is found in Jeremiah 4:1-4, and it states two important things:

> ¹ *If thou will return, O Israel, saith the LORD, return unto me: and if thou will put away your abominations out of my sight, then shall you not be removed.*
> ² *And you shall swear, the LORD liveth* [lives], *in truth, in judgment, and in righteousness; and* **the nations shall bless themselves in him** *and* **in him shall they glory.**
> ³ *For thus saith* [says] *the LORD to the men of Judah and Jerusalem, break up your fallow ground, and sow not among thorns.*
> ⁴ **Circumcise yourselves to the *LORD*, and take away the foreskins of your heart,** *you men of Judah and inhabitants of Jerusalem: lest my fury come forth like a fire, and burn that none can quench it, because of the evil of your doings.*

In verse 2 Jeremiah states that *the nations shall bless themselves in him,* a third person pronoun. This is a reference back to the Abrahamic Covenant in Genesis 12:3 where it states that through Abraham—and particularly in the singular **Seed** of Abraham—a*ll the families of the earth will be blessed*, including Israel. This is a promise to the 70 nations of Genesis 10 and all the peoples that have come through them: in other words, all the Gentiles in the future of Jeremiah's writing will be blessed by this **Seed**. But the question is, "Who is it that they bless themselves in?" Who is the *in him*? The *in him* is not the nation of Israel. It also says that *in him shall they* [the Gentiles] *glory*. This is the same person or **Seed**, the Messiah that Isaiah spoke of as a *light to the Gentiles* in Isaiah 42:6 and 49:6 and the one who would restore Jacob from sin and separation from *HaShem*.

I have not said too much about the theme of Blessing, but the **Seed** of Abraham, that will be the **King** of Judah, the **Prophet** like Moses, the son of David born of a virgin, who is named by *HaShem* with names that only apply to *Elokim* it is He who will be a **Blessing** to Israel in particular, but also to the Gentiles.

Jeremiah 4:4 also refers to Moses' plea (Deuteronomy 10:16; 30:6) that the people of Israel [Judah] which included the other 10 tribes which had immigrated to Judah from the religious and political corruption of the 10 northern tribes are to circumcise their hearts.

Why? Because both Israel and Judah had broken the Mosaic Covenant made between them and *HaShem* at Mt. Sinai. When Jeremiah wrote, only Judah was in existence; Israel had already gone into captivity. They did not walk in His commandment, statutes and ordinances (Jeremiah 31:31-34 [30-33]). Israel [Judah] needed to circumcise the foreskin of their *flesh* in obedience first to the Abrahamic Covenant (Genesis 17:9-14) as well as to the Mosaic Covenant to which Israel has been unfaithful. Jeremiah points out Israel's unfaithfulness in Jeremiah 9:26 [25] when *HaShem* equates Israel with the uncircumcised neighboring nations. *HaShem* states the following:

> *...for all these nations are uncircumcised, and all the house of Israel are uncircumcised in the heart.*

Jeremiah has been reading Moses for he said that Israel's heart was uncircumcised (unregenerate) and until it was, Israel would have trouble obeying the *Sh'ma* because they did not *love the LORD their God with all their heart* (Deuteronomy 6:5; 30:6).

Jeremiah 23:5-6

In the next passage Jeremiah spoke to the fact that this **Seed** will be from David's family, and Jeremiah references Him as being righteous as a quality of His being. In fact Jeremiah says that this *righteous BRANCH* is named by *HaShem* as *THE LORD OUR RIGHTEOUSNESS*. Obviously the **Seed** promised would have to be both man (a descendant of David) and divine *(THE LORD OUR RIGHTEOUSNESS)*. This passage focuses on the **Seed** as the **King**, the son of David who is by His character righteous. No man or woman for that matter is righteous by their character, yet here is a promised son of David who is a man and yet by character He is named by *HaShem* as *THE LORD OUR RIGHTEOUSNESS*. The G-d/man concept here is clear. Remember that is exactly what Eve understood when she gave birth in Genesis 4:1 to her first born son, *I have begotten a man, the LORD*. This is hard to believe, but this is exactly what *HaShem* Himself is saying through the prophets. Look at the verse in Jeremiah 23:5-6:

> *⁵ Behold the days come, saith* [says] *the LORD, that I will raise* **unto David a righteous Branch,** *and a King shall reign and prosper, and shall execute judgment and justice in the earth.* *⁶ in his days Judah shall be saved, and Israel shall dwell safely: and this is his name whereby* **he shall be called, THE *LORD*** [is] **OUR RIGHTEOUSNESS.**

Once again this passage is diluted because the rabbis have added the word *is* into the name for the purpose of making the **King** less than He is; on the contrary, *THE LORD OUR RIGHTEOUSNESS* is a name and not a description. Notice as well it is the *L-RD* not man who names the King thus. This passage primarily refers to the Messianic Kingdom to come, but it also reveals this righteous BRANCH to be the son of David in agreement with the Davidic Covenant. The righteousness that He has is not an acquired righteousness; He *is* RIGHTEOUSNESS by character, which His name declares.

Prophet Micah

As we move on, the prophet Micah, who was a contemporary of Isaiah, gives a very unusual statement concerning the origin and place of birth of the **Seed**, the **King**, the **Prophet**, who is the son of David, the King of Righteousness. Look carefully at Micah 5:2[1]:

> *And you,* **O Bethlehem of Ephrath,** *least among the clans of Judah, out of you one shall come forth unto me that is to be ruler in Israel,* **whose goings forth are from of old, from everlasting.**

As we look at this verse it becomes increasingly apparent that one prophet after another is building upon the revealed Word of *Elokim*. Here the prophet states that the Promised One will be born in Bethlehem of Judah and that He, the Messiah, is from everlasting. Rabbinic Judaism of today tries to say that it means his origin is from Bethlehem and not physically born or coming from Bethlehem personally. That is a problem for them on two accounts:

- First, they contradict the sages of old that said the Messiah would be born in Bethlehem.

- Second, today you know Bethlehem is an Arab and mostly Moslem town and there are no longer Jewish people living there. And if the Israelis allow a Palestinian State in the West Bank there is no possibility of a future Jewish Messiah coming from Bethlehem anytime soon. So if the Messiah is coming in the near future, how can He be born there? However, all the sages of the past with one voice said that the Messiah will be born in Bethlehem.

Why does rabbinic Judaism change the interpretation of *HaShem*'s clearly written Word? Because Jesus whose Hebrew name is *Yeshua* was born there, and they absolutely do not want any verse that would support the fact that the Messiah must be born there. Micah says a Jewish woman from the house of David will give birth to the Messiah in Bethlehem.[41] That is not possible today; first because Bethlehem is a Moslem town; and secondly, because no Jewish person today can trace his or her tribal identity from the house of David. For the Messiah to come from Bethlehem today as well has having proof that he is of David is simply not possible, unless he has already come.

Prophet Zechariah

Zechariah is another exceptional book, like the Book of Isaiah that has many points that speak of the Messiah. There are numerous passages that could be cited, but we will only look at four of them. The first passage will be from Zechariah 11:12-13, but the wider context is verses 4:14:

Zechariah 11:12-13

[12] And I [LORD] said unto them, If you think good, **give my price;** *and if not, forbear. So they weighed for my* **price thirty pieces of silver.** *[13] And the LORD said unto me [Zechariah], Cast it unto the potter:* **a goodly price that I was prised** [apprised] **at of them.** *And I took the thirty pieces of silver,*

---

[41] See the New Testament Gospel of Matthew 2:1-6.

and cast them to the potter **in the house of the LORD.**

Zechariah is a post-exile prophet writing sometime in the late 6th to 5th century BCE. In verse 4 the speaker is *HaShem* and has presented Himself as the Shepherd of Israel, to His flock of sheep to which He has been ministering. Then in verse 12, based on His ministry to them, He asked for His wages. He was not looking for money but for their obedience to His law, with love and devotion for Him. But instead they valued Him for 30 pieces of silver. *HaShem* responds with a bit of sarcasm, *a goodly price that I was prised at of them.* Then Zechariah who was acting out this story is told to cast the thirty pieces of silver, into *the house of the LORD.* This was an act of betrayal by Israel and an insult directed toward *HaShem.* But there is something else, for the 30 pieces has a reference to the Mosaic Law. In Exodus 21:32, if an ox of one owner kills a slave belonging to another master, he is obligated to pay that slave owner 30 pieces of silver for the dead slave. So here in Zechariah *HaShem* is valued by the leadership of Israel as no more to them than a dead slave. Thirty pieces of silver was an insult directed to *HaShem* and His personal ministry to Israel. There is a connection between this passage in the prophets to the ministry of *Yeshua* in the gospel account in the New Testament.[42] Here *HaShem* wants an intimate relationship with His people[43] and is rebuffed and rejected by them. This is a prophecy given over 500 years before its fulfillment. The *Tanakh* speaks to the rejection of the leadership of the Messiah, the Seed, the King, son of David who was the Prophet promised by *HaShem* in Deuteronomy 18:15-19.

---

[42] See the Gospel of Matthew in the New Testament in 26:14-16; 27:3-9.
[43] See the Gospel of Matthew in the New Testament in 23:37-39.

This rejection will also be seen in the next verse from Zechariah.

Zechariah 12:1, 10

The next passage is found in Zechariah 12:1, 10, which states the following:

> [1] *The burden of the word of the LORD for Israel,* **saith** [says] **the *LORD,*** *which stretcheth forth the heavens, and layeth the foundation of the earth, and formeth the spirit of man within him.*
>
> [10] *And I will pour upon the house of David, and upon the inhabitants of Jerusalem, the spirit of grace and of supplications:* **and they shall look upon me whom they have pierced,** *and* **they shall mourn for him,** *as one mourneth for his only son, and shall be in bitterness for him, as one that is in bitterness for his first born.*

The speaker in verse 1 is *HaShem* who is the one who stretched out the heavens and laid the foundations of the earth and formed the spirit of man. This is the same Person who spoke as the Sent One in Isaiah 48:16 who identified Himself as the One who called Israel, He is the First and the Last as well as the Creator in Isaiah 48:12-13. This plurality of *Elokim* that He sets forth of Himself is revealed as well in Ecclesiastes 12:1 where He calls on Israel to remember their Creator, which is a plural word. Here in Zechariah He is speaking to Israel in the context of the last days, which I believe we are approaching for the "Footsteps of Messiah" can be heard.

Now rabbinic Judaism is correct when they say that the words of the Hebrew text have not been altered. In this they are correct. However, there is an issue with the vowel pointings of the Masoretes around 900 CE. To be completely fair, their vowel pointings are usually very helpful in the study and reading of the Hebrew text. But as a result of their interaction with christianity for 800 plus years, some of the vowel pointings reflect a bias against New Testament believers and their interpretation of Messianic passages. They also go against the Messianic passages and show a bias against the Septuagint which was a translation by the Rabbis 250 years before the New Testament era. The Septuagint is not an invention of true believers in Messiah, but of Rabbis before *Yeshua* was an issue. The vowel pointings are not sacred Scripture, and an anti-Messianic bias comes out in several passages, one of which is Zechariah 12:10. By making certain vowel pointings, one can change the meaning of the text. To illustrate, Zechariah 12:10 in the Jewish Bible reads *they shall look* **unto** *me* ***for every one*** *whom they have pierced.* Two things should be noted: The words "for every one" are in italics which means the wording is not in the original text but has been added. In most cases additions like that are helpful in the flow of grammar and thought, but not here. Also there is a slight change in the vowel pointings; the word *upon* becomes "unto," changing the verse from an act taken against *HaShem* to the action being taken against others.

In the second part of the verse there is confusion for most readers involving the changing [of] pronouns in this passage. First in verse 12 you have the pronoun *they* used twice, both times referring to Israel. But to whom do the other two pronouns *me* and *him* refer? The main issue for Jewish scholars is how to resolve the changing of the pronouns that G-d used of Himself, from "*me*" to "*him*" in this passage. This shift in the pronouns goes from *HaShem* as first person, "*me*," to the one who is mourned for in the

127

third person, as "*him*." The lament for *HaShem* who was pierced through is viewed from *HaShem*'s perspective as "*me*," whereas the "*him*" is viewed from a future generation of Jewish people who will recognize *HaShem* as "*him*" the one they were responsible for piercing. So from *HaShem*'s viewpoint it is "*me*" that is the focus and from the people it is "*him*."

Continuing our thought on verse 10, He states that He is personally pierced. Now G-d is spirit so how can He be pierced? Yet He describes something that happened to him as was also described in Isaiah 50:4-6 where He was scourged, spit upon, and His beard of pulled out of His face. In both instances *HaShem* is referring to something that could only happen if He was in a body of flesh. This idea rabbinic Judaism flees from with all kinds of creative reasoning because of what *HaShem* is saying. In English translations they try very hard to remove the emphasis that *HaShem* Himself places on the text. In the *Talmud* they attempt as another argument to explain the phrase in Zechariah 12:10 away by saying that it was the evil inclination that was pierced, but that is not anywhere in the context. Another attempt is made to say that Israel is lamenting to *HaShem* for those who are slain on the Day of the *L-RD*. But once again *HaShem* states that it personally happened to Him.

Rabbinic Judaism dislikes this verse for two reasons: First it implies that *HaShem* has taken on a body of flesh, which is exactly what Moses and the prophets, Isaiah, Micah, Jeremiah, and now Zechariah are saying. It coincides with the first text that we looked at, the central theme that runs through the *Tanakh*, which was first given in Genesis 3:15: namely, the **Seed** of the woman is the focus. Secondly, it coincides with the crucifixion of *Yeshua* in the

New Testament. Could it be possible that *HaShem became flesh and dwelt among us*?[44] The prophets pointed to this G-d/man who would be the Messiah.

The **Seed** according to Genesis 3:15 will suffer a wound in the heel from Satan. When the Kingdom was presented to Israel by the **King** Messiah, He was rejected. The Prophet that was promised by *HaShem* in Deuteronomy 18:18-19 who would speak the words of *HaShem* will be rebuffed and rejected. Let us view the continuing theme of Zechariah as to the rejection of the *Mashiach* by Israel's first century religious leadership.

Zechariah 13:7

Zechariah continues his presentation of the G-d/man concept in Zechariah 13:7:

> *Awake,* **O sword, against my shepherd,** *and* **against the man my fellow,** *saith* [says] *the LORD of hosts:* **smite the shepherd,** *and the sheep shall be scattered: and I will turn mine hand upon the little ones.*

This gets hard to grasp. Here Zechariah states *HaShem*'s command for an instrument of death to arise against *my shepherd*, which also directly refers to *HaShem* who is also Israel's Shepherd in Zechariah 11:4-14. He calls for the sword to go against His very own shepherd. Reread those passages again in Zechariah 11-12. Then *HaShem* referencing the *same person* calls for the sword to be not only against His shepherd but against the man who is His fellow. The word for *fellow* means someone who is His equal. It is used only eleven times in the *Tanakh*, once here

---

[44] See the Gospel of John in the New Testament, John 1:1-14.

in Zechariah and all the other times in Moses' Book of Leviticus where it refers to men who are the equal to other men. So *HaShem* is calling for the sword to arise against His shepherd, against the man who is His equal! Again Zechariah is picking up on the concept and theme that has been running throughout the *Tanakh* and that is stated in Genesis 3:15. The **Seed** of the woman will be the G-d/man. Then *HaShem* commands the sword to kill the shepherd. Notice who takes personal responsibility for the death of the shepherd: *HaShem* does! This is exactly what transpired in the New Testament record when the rabbis of the day wanted this itinerant rabbi called *Yeshua* [Jesus] removed, because he was a threat to them and to their authority. They cooperated with Pilate, who represented Rome, to have him crucified; yet *HaShem* takes full responsibility for the death of Messiah.

Zechariah 14:3-4

The last verse that I will reference in Zechariah is a passage that I had read over and not seen what *HaShem* was saying about Himself. It speaks of the days just before the return of *HaShem* to rescue and deliver Israel from the armies that are bent on annihilating all of the Jewish people from off the earth. *HaShem* personally comes and fights for Israel, but also notice another unexpected phrase about *HaShem*.

> *3 Then shall the **LORD** go forth, and fight against those nations, as when he fought in the day of battle.*
> *4 And **his feet shall stand in that day upon the mount of Olives** which is before Jerusalem on the east, and the mount of Olives shall cleave in the midst thereof toward the east and toward the west, and there shall be a very great valley; and half of*

the mountain shall remove toward the north, and half of it toward the south.

In verse 3 *HaShem* moves against Israel's enemies. But in verse 4 it states that ***his feet*** *shall stand in that day upon the Mount of Olives*. Who's feet? *HaShem*'s feet, but *HaShem* is pure Spirit and does not have a body! It is true, but look back to Exodus 24:9-11 where Moses and seventy of the Elders of Israel saw the *L-RD*; the only part that Moses describes as to what they saw was the platform that *HaShem* stood on and *HaShem*'s feet. Here is another verse that points to what the prophets have been saying since Moses. The **Seed** of the woman from Judah, this son (descendant) of David has been revealed as G-d coming in the flesh. The same was revealed by G-d via Moses, Nathan, Isaiah, Jeremiah, Micah and Zechariah. The Messiah of Israel was prophesied to come as *Elokim* in flesh, and He came to Israel as a child, but the son given was from *HaShem* as Isaiah 9:6-7 [5-6] stated.

The Prophet Malachi

Malachi, the last of the prophets, also has something to say. Malachi wrote in the late 5th century BCE. In Malachi 3:1 he states the following:

> *Behold,* **I will send my messenger,** *and* **he** *shall prepare the way* **before me:** *and* **the Lord, whom you seek, shall suddenly come to his temple, even the messenger of the covenant,** *whom you delight in: behold, he shall come, saith* [says] *the LORD of hosts.*

In this verse you have two persons mentioned, first **the Messenger** who will *prepare the way before me*. This is not Elijah but the ministry of John the Baptist at Messiah's first coming.[45] Second, **The *Lord***, *Adhonai*, Israel's Master, will come to **His** temple. Does Malachi say that is literal or figurative? If you think that it is figurative, then explain how *HaShem* came to dwell in the tabernacle in Exodus 40 and Solomon's Temple in 1 Kings 8:10-11 but did not come in the same manner during the second temple period. Both Exodus 40 and I Kings 8 were literal, so why should not this be literal as well? Another interpretation issue arises with this passage in that it refers to the second temple period which involves Zerubbabel's Temple and Herod's refurbishing of that temple. Judaism has no reference either talmudicly or in Midrash commentaries to confirm that any such appearance happened during the second temple period. But the prophets have been speaking of the **Seed** coming in flesh and of an unnamed herald according to this passage and Isaiah 40:3. That is exactly what John the Baptist did as the herald of *Yeshua* when *Adhonai* came to His temple fulfilling Malachi 3:1. He showed Himself at the second temple. Let us now go back to Malachi 3:1.

Malachi clarifies who the L-rd is when he says *even the messenger of the covenant*. The word *suddenly* when used in the *Tanakh* (used 25 times) is used in every passage to mean coming disaster and judgment. Who then is *the messenger of the covenant* who will come suddenly? This is a reference back to the Mosaic Law, and the one who gave the Law to Moses is *Elokim*, *HaShem*, the *Shechinah* glory of *HaShem*, *the angel of the LORD* who has the very name of *HaShem* in Him, who also received worship and spoke as *Elokim* or *HaShem* Himself. Finally the speaker identifies Himself in this verse as *Adhonai*, the L-rd. Notice *Adhonai* will come

---

[45] See the four New Testament Gospels of John, Matthew, Mark, and Luke: John 1:6-8, 15-34; Matthew 3:1-17; Mark 1:1-11; Luke 3:1-20.

to **His** temple, and He is described as *the messenger of the covenant.* These are difficult verses to understand because rabbinic Judaism over the centuries has painted a picture of *Yeshua* as a worthless rabbi who claimed to be *HaShem* and needed to be removed. But why reject *Yeshua*? First, Jesus claimed to be G-d.[46] Secondly, He attacked them at the core of their authority, their rabbinic man-made laws. So today they claim that the church concocted His deity 300 years after He lived. This is entirely erroneous for the original writing of the believers in *Yeshua* were all written within 40 years of the death and resurrection of *Yeshua*, except for the writings of Apostle John who wrote in the late 1st century CE. He was also an eye witness of the life and ministry of *Yeshua*. So it is good to look at the New Testament when it was written, not 300 hundred years later when the church fathers began to corrupt the teaching of *Yeshua* and His Apostles.

When we finished reviewing the Books of Moses we looked at the last four verses of Deuteronomy and saw that throughout Israel's history there had not arisen a **Prophet** *like unto Moses.* Now at the end of the Prophets section of the *Tanakh* we also see that they were still looking for the Messiah, the **Seed** of the woman; but before He would return and deliver Israel and set up the Kingdom, the prophet Elijah here named would precede Him, as stated in Malachi 4:4-6: [3:22-24]

> *⁴ Remember you the law of Moses my servant, which I commanded unto him in Horeb for all Israel, with the statues and judgments. ⁵ Behold, I will send you Elijah the prophet before the coming of the great and dreadful day of the LORD: ⁶ And he shall turn*

---

[46] See the New Testament Gospel of John: 8:54-59; 10:30-33

the heart of the fathers to the children, and the heart
of the children to their fathers, lest I come and smite
the earth with a curse.

Malachi speaks of two heralds coming; the unnamed herald of Malachi 3:1 who would introduce Messiah to Israel in the first century CE and Elijah who will fulfill the passage above in the future. Once again you have a reference to Moses my servant and his law. The **Prophet** like Moses had not come but he would be preceded before the *great and dreadful day of the LORD* by Elijah. Even in the Passover Seder the youngest boy who asks the four questions will later go to the door to see if the special guest Elijah is coming. Elijah will come to turn the hearts of the children to their parents because in the first coming of Messiah the leadership made Jesus a *stone of stumbling* as stated in Isaiah 8:14:

> *And he shall be for a sanctuary; but for a stone of*
> *stumbling and for a rock of offence to both the*
> *houses of Israel, for a gin* [a snare or trap] *and for a*
> *snare to the inhabitants of Jerusalem.* [Brackets are mine.]

Here Isaiah is referencing Immanuel, *God With Us*, who would become the point of division in the Jewish family structure. *Yeshua* became the *rock of offence* to the Jewish family structure whenever a division occurred in the Jewish family over the Messiahship of *Yeshua*. The **Seed, King** and **Prophet** has become a dividing point between Jewish family members. Moses in initiating the themes of the **Seed**, **King** and **Prophet** did not show that division, but as *HaShem* wrote through the prophets like Isaiah, Jeremiah, Daniel, Zechariah and Micah, that rejection and division becomes an open source of contention.

134

Yeshua in coming to the temple, the second temple, claimed that He was *HaShem* the **Seed**, the **King**, son of David, Immanuel and the **Prophet** in flesh who would be a **Blessing** as prophesied to the whole world.[47] Now at this point in time, Elijah has not come; however, a close study of the *Tanakh* shows us that the *great and dreadful day of the LORD* is not far removed from us. If that is so, then *Yeshua* will return as He declared He would, to intervene at a critical juncture. For this second return, Elijah is to be the herald, as the prophets revealed. Gird up yourselves, Israel, for dreadful days are approaching; the storm clouds are coming, and *the time of Jacob's trouble* is approaching which also could be called the second holocaust. The returning "footsteps of the Messiah" can be heard if you are listening

---

[47] See these New Testament Gospel passages: John 1:18; 5:39, 46; Luke 24:25-27, 44; Matthew 23:37-39.

Chapter Nine:
Messiah: Seed, King and Prophet in the Writings

If you remember when we began the Prophet section we said that there are connections—seams or hinges—between the sections of the *Tanakh*. We saw the connection between the Law and the Prophets in Joshua 1:8, where G-d's people are directed to meditate on the Written Law of *HaShem* and receive His blessings.

Now in the last section of the Hebrew Scriptures there is another connection between the Written Law and the Writings, just as there was between the Law and the Prophets, and the theme is the same: Meditate on the Law and walk in the Law uprightly before your G-d. See the words of the Psalmist in Psalm 1:

> *¹ Blessed is the man that walks not in the counsel of the ungodly, nor stands in the way of sinners, nor sits in the seat of the scornful. ² But* **his delight is in the Law of the *LORD*;** *and* **in his law doth he meditate day and night.**

I do not need to make too many comments on this passage for it is self-explanatory. This passage is just like an expanded statement of what *HaShem* said to Joshua. Here is a statement to all of Israel, for it is the first chapter or song in the hymnal of Israel—the Psalms.—the first book in the Writings section of the *Tanakh*.

David's Last Words - 2 Sam 23:1-5a

Even though this passage is in the Prophets, it has a direct bearing on the Psalms, and we need to observe it carefully. Here is the passage:

> *[1] Now these be the last words of David. David the son of Jesse said, and the man who was raised up* **on high,** *the anointed of the God of Jacob, and the sweet psalmist of Israel, said,*
> *[2] The Spirit of the LORD spoke by me, and his word was upon my tongue.*
> *[3] The God of Israel said, the Rock of Israel spoke to me, He that ruleth over men must be just, ruling in the fear of God.*
> *[4] And he shall be as the light of the morning, when the sun rises, even a morning without clouds; as the tender grass springing out of the earth by clear shining after rain.*
> *[5] Is not so my house with God? Yet he hath made with me an everlasting covenant, ...*

In this veiled passage we are dealing with vowel pointings in the Masoretic text, and it must be remembered that the vowel pointings are not part of Scripture but added by the Masoretes who had also been dealing with Christian teaching about Jesus for 900 years. What you have here is David's last words as he reflected back to the Davidic Covenant and on the Psalms he had written and the subject of those Psalms: the Anointed One, the Messiah. He states that the Holy Spirit and *Elokim* his Rock spoke to him concerning the Messiah that he had written about in the Psalms. Upon entering the Psalms we need to understand that the subject of David's psalms was the *Anointed* One that *HaShem* promised through Moses and Nathan in Davidic Covenant. Depending on the vowel pointings, the words *on high* could be translated *concerning the anointed of the God of Jacob*. In fact once again the Septuagint sheds light on the subject. For the Septuagint uses the word "concerning" and not the words "on high." Also remember that the Septuagint was translated 1,000 years before the Masoretes and before *Yeshua* was born. This rendering of the passage sheds far more light on the Messianic passages and Psalms that David wrote.

Also in verse 5 once again the vowel pointings are important; but here the two different translations are at complete odds. It is either David saying *although my house is not so with God*, or, *is not my house with God?* David was a man after G-d's own heart, but David's house was a house of division with conflict after conflict. David personally was a man after *HaShem*'s heart, but his house was full of tension, strife, hatred, envy and mutiny. In reviewing the psalms of David, we understand that **he was writing about** the Anointed of Israel, a future son of David, the Messiah. There are many psalms in which he speaks of the Messiah, such as Psalms 2, 16, 22 24, 29, 40, 42-48, 50, 63, 72, 110 and 118 but we will only look at five of them.

We will be looking at seven passages in the Writings section of the *Tanakh*, five of which will be in the Psalms, one in the Book of Proverbs and the last in the Book of Daniel. What do the Writings say about Messiah?

Psalm 2

¹ Why do the heathen rage, and the people imagine a vain thing?

² The kings of the earth set themselves, and the rulers take counsel together, **against the *LORD*,** *and* **against His anointed,** *saying,*

³ Let us break their bands asunder, and cast away their cords from us.

⁴ He that sitteth in the heavens shall laugh: the Lord shall have them in derision.

⁵ Then shall he speak unto them in his wrath, and vex them in his sore displeasure.

⁶ Yet have I set **my king** *upon my holy hill of Zion.*

⁷ I will declare the decree: the LORD hath said unto me, Thou art **my Son;** *this day have I begotten thee.*

⁸ Ask of me, and I shall give you the heathen for thine [your] *inheritance,* **and the uttermost parts of the earth for your possession.**

⁹ You shall break them with a rod of iron; you shall dash them in pieces like a potter's vessel.

¹⁰ Be wise now therefore, O you kings: be instructed, you judges of the earth.

¹¹ **Serve the *LORD*** *with fear, and rejoice with trembling.*

¹² **Kiss the Son,** *lest he be angry, and you perish from the way, when his wrath is kindled by a little. Blessed are all they that put their trust in him.*

This psalm has been recognized by the sages as a psalm of David as well as a Messianic Psalm. It is a Psalm concerning the anointed of Jacob, the Messiah. Verses 1 and 2 point out that the kings of the earth join together to throw off the rule of the *Anointed* who reigns. It is an act against *HaShem* and against *His Anointed*. *HaShem* will laugh at them with a scornful, mocking laugh before His wrath falls on them. In verse 6 the *Anointed* of *HaShem* is *My king* whom He has placed on His holy hill This is a direct connection of David to the King theme that Moses developed in Genesis 49:10 and Numbers 24:9, 17. In verse 7 *HaShem* calls the King *My Son*, and *HaShem* will give to Him, His Son, the *uttermost parts of the earth* as His possession which is referenced in Isaiah 9:6-7 [5-6]. This passage also has a parallel to Proverbs 30:4, which speaks of G-d's Son. Once again the theme goes back to Moses concerning the **King** that was developed by the Davidic Covenant and elaborated upon in the Prophets. The **Seed** of the woman would come from a miraculous birth as the **King**, and the **Prophet**. This **Seed** would be a singular individual that Israel called the *Anointed*, the Messiah, who would not only restore Jacob (Isaiah 49:5), but restore the earth so that a wolf will feed with the lamb, a child will play safely at the hole of a poisons snake, and men will cast away their swords and make them into plows to harvest the abundance of food (Isaiah 2:4; 11:8; 65:25). *HaShem* is saying to the rulers of the earth, "If you are smart you will submit to *My Son* and pay homage to the Son, showing reverence and fear to His person."   This is truly an interesting Psalm as the Son is viewed as equal to the Father.

Psalm 16

Let us now look at Psalm 16:10-11 and see what it has to say:

> *10 For thou will* **not commit my soul to the grave; neither will you suffer your Holy One to see corruption.** *11 You will show me the path of life: in thy presence is fullness of joy;* **at your right hand** *there are pleasures for evermore.*

Psalm 16 is a psalm and prayer of David and is commonly recognized as a Messianic Psalm. We will only look at verses 10-11. David is speaking prophetically of the Messiah when he says *Elokim will not leave my soul in hell*, which is a promise of a resurrection. Then he says neither will *Elokim* allow His Holy One to see corruption. This is not only resurrection, but resurrection before the body decays. That cannot possibly be referring to David, for his tomb is yet with us; it must reference someone else, such as the Messiah who would be scourged (Isaiah 50:4-6) and pierced (Zechariah 12:10) and be put to death or cut off (Isaiah 53:8; Daniel 9:26). Then in the next verse this Holy One who will not see corruption will be at *HaShem*'s right hand, and that is a position of equality. So the Messiah will die, be resurrected within three days before His body sees corruption,[48] and He will be at the right hand of *HaShem* (Psalms 80:17 [18]; Isaiah 62:8). As can be clearly seen in this psalm of David, he is not referring to himself but to the Messiah. Notice that to die and potentially see corruption and be resurrected can only happen to a human being, but this human being, the **Seed** of the woman, will be at *HaShem*'s right hand until *HaShem* makes the earth His footstool (Psalm 110:1). Here David is pointing to the Messiah who is G-d, for He will sit at the right hand of *HaShem*, the place of equality, and His death and resurrection speak to His humanity.

Psalm 22

Next we look at Psalm 22, which is another psalm of David that is referencing the Messiah. Let us look at verses 14-18 [15-19]:

---

[48] See these New Testament Gospel passages: Matthew 12:38-39 with John 11:38-44; Acts 2:25-31; 13:35

[14] *I am* **poured out like water,** *and* **all my bones are out of joint:** *my* **heart is like wax;** *it is melted in the midst of my bowels.* *[15]* **My strength is dried up like a potsherd;** *and* **my tongue cleaveth to my jaws;** *and* **thou hast brought me into the dust of death.** *[16]* *For* **dogs have compassed me:** *the* **assembly of the wicked have inclosed me: they pierced my hands and my feet.** *[17]* *I* **may tell all my bones: they look and stare upon me.** *[18]* **They part my garments among them,** *and* **cast lots upon my vesture.**

This passage written by David concerning the Messiah was written hundreds of years before Rome even came into existence and used crucifixion as their form of capital punishment. This passage is the mirror image of the crucifixion of *Yeshua*, who was a son of David, Immanuel who presented Himself to Israel as their promised Messiah, the **Seed** of the woman, Abraham, Judah, David, born of a virgin, in the city of Bethlehem. But they rejected him and valued Him as nothing more than a dead slave (30 pieces of silver – Zechariah 11:12-13). He is presently sitting at *HaShem*'s right hand and will come riding on the clouds of heaven (Daniel 7:13-14).[49]

To explain away the prophecy in Psalm 22, rabbinic Judaism will use the reading from the Masoretic Text with their vowel pointings which says "like a lion, my hands and my feet" instead of *they pierced my hands and my feet*. However, the Septuagint (250 BCE), which predates the Masoretic text (900 CE) by well over 1000 years, says *they pierced my hands and my feet*. This was **rendered** 250 years before *Yeshua* was an issue.

---

[49] Compare with the Gospel of Matthew chapter 26, verses 63-68.

The Septuagint was the standard Bible for all Greek-speaking Jewish people leading up to the second century CE, having been translated by rabbis into the Greek. Recall that the vowel markings in the Masoretic text are not inspired but placed there almost 900 years after the first century. They are often very helpful, but in this case they reflect an unfounded rabbinic bias against *Yeshua* being the Messiah. The Messiah that David spoke of in Psalm 22 was to redeem this sin-corrupted world made up of both Jews and Gentiles to restore the fellowship lost at the sin of Adam and Eve in the Garden of Eden (Genesis 3). The close description in Psalm 22 of the tortuous death of Immanuel provides us with another connection point regarding the identity of Messiah.

Psalm 80:17 [18]

The next psalm is a psalm of Asaph and is another Messianic psalm. Look with me at just verse 17 of Psalm 80:

Let your hand be upon **the man of thy right hand,**
upon the son of man you made strong for yourself.

Once again you have a reference of a man who is called *the man of thy right hand.* To be at the right hand of *HaShem* you must be equal to *HaShem* because the right hand shows all the power and strength of *HaShem.* Here He is referred to as a man which is what Zechariah also states in Zechariah 6:12-13; 13:7 as well as Isaiah 9:6-7 [5-6]; 7:14; 11:1-2; 52:13-53:12; Micah 5:2 [1]; Jeremiah 23:5-6. Rabbinic Judaism vigorously rejects the incarnation of *HaShem.* Yet what we are seeing in these passages can only be the incarnation of *HaShem* coming into His world as a man, born in Bethlehem of the tribe of Judah, and son of

David to fulfill the original prophecy given by *HaShem* in Genesis 3:15 and explained in Isaiah 7:14.

Psalm 110

This passage is unique for there are three Individuals involved in this text. Let us look together at another Messianic psalm of David from Psalm 110:1-4 and see what David says:

> *¹ The **LORD** [HaShem] **said unto my Lord** [Adoni], Sit thou **at my right hand,** until I make thine [your] enemies your footstool, ² The **LORD** [HaShem] shall send the rod of your strength out of Zion: rule thou in the midst of **thine** [your] **enemies**. ³ Thy people shall be willing in the day of your power, in the beauties of holiness from the womb of the morning: you have the dew of thy youth. ⁴ **The LORD** [HaShem] **hath sworn,** and will not repent, **You** [Adoni] **are a priest for ever after the order of Melchizedek.***

You have in the first phrase of verse one David speaking of the plurality of *Elokim* in that *HaShem* is speaking to *Adoni*. At the same time you have three personalities being referenced, *HaShem*, David and *Adoni*. David as king had no human lord, but David the writer, speaks of *Adoni* as **my Lord**. So who is Adoni? The reference to *HaShem* and *Adoni* clearly show the plurality of G-d and *Adoni* is understood to be the Messiah in this context. David quotes *HaShem* as saying to *Adoni*, **sit thou at my right hand,** which is the position of equality with *HaShem*. What is being pictured here by David is the plurality of *Elokim*.

What has already been demonstrated in this book is that *HaShem* and Israel are enemies even through that is not the theme of this book. *HaShem* has said in Leviticus 26:24, 28, 41 that if Israel walked contrary to His Law, He would walk contrary to them because they have abhorred His Law (verse 43). So why does *HaShem* say to *Adoni*, *"Sit at my right hand until I make your enemies His footstool"*?

- To whom was the Messiah to come?

- Whom did Israel reject when He came to His temple?

- Who rejected the Suffering Servant of Isaiah 53?

- Who rejected the Seed that was promised?

- Who rejected their King, the son of David?

- Who rejected the Prophet like unto Moses?

- Why did *HaShem* divorce Israel in the Book of Hosea?

- Why did *HaShem* divorce Judah in the Book of Jeremiah?

Many verses from the *Tanakh* can be supplied to show that Israel would go after other gods, abhor His Law and ultimately reject the Messiah, son of David, Immanuel, the Branch. Israel has chosen to be in an active state of rebellion against *HaShem*. You may say that is not true, but then why is *HaShem* silent to His people, His first-born? Why are most Jewish people living in the nations of the Gentiles suffering at the hands of the Gentiles for 2,000 years instead of living in Israel? I do not have to go into detail of all that has been charged against Israel and has been perpetrated against Israel by heathen christian Gentiles.

146

The fact that Israel has been an enemy of *HaShem* is difficult to grasp, but history and the Hebrew Scriptures verify that fact. So *Adoni*, the Messiah, has an unexpected enemy in the nation of Israel, His own chosen people, and Israel has the nations of the Gentiles as enemies. In the future when Israel repents (Isaiah 53, Leviticus 26:40; Hosea 5:15) about the identity of the Messiah, He will come and deliver them. At that point in the future Israel will not be an enemy of Messiah because the Messiah will fulfill the New Covenant and circumcise their hearts, regenerate their hearts and will come and destroy all of Israel's Gentile enemies.

This is another text that causes a real issue with rabbinic Judaism which believes that *HaShem* who at other times is called *Adoni* as well as *Elokim* as an absolute one (*yachid*) when *HaShem*'s word clearly makes them all completely equal with each other, one (*echad*).

Beyond that, we see that David's L-rd in verse 4 is called by *HaShem a priest forever*. That is forbidden under the Mosaic Law. A son of David of the tribe of Judah cannot be or function as a Levitical priest, but He can function as a Melchizedekian priest. Messiah is stated to be *of the order of Melchizedek*; that is, of a different order of priests. According to Zechariah, this Messiah will be different in that he will be a priest who rules from his throne (Zechariah 6:12-13). David explains how this exception will occur, by identifying Him as *of the order of Melchizedek*, who was the King of Salem (Jerusalem) and priest of *El Elyon* (G-d Most High), who blessed Abraham long before the Levitical priesthood even existed.

This is another text that causes a real issue with rabbinic Judaism which believes that *HaShem* who at other times is called *Adoni* as well as *Elokim* is an absolute one (*yachid*) when *HaShem*'s Word clearly makes them all completely equal with each other, one (*echad*).

In summary the *Tanakh* keeps on filling in the pieces of the puzzle as to the identity of the Messiah, the Seed or the Promised One, the King who is the son of David and the Prophet who will be *like Moses*. If the *Sh'ma* had been practiced, He would have been seen by His people but instead, the failure to Love the *L-RD* G-D and His Written Word with all their heart was neglected.

Proverb 30:4

In this passage from the Book of Proverbs come several very perplexing rhetorical questions. These questions have very easy answers with the exception of the last one. Please view Proverbs 30:4 with me:

> **Who** *hath ascended up into heaven, or descended? Who hath gathered the wind in his fists?* **Who** *hath bound the waters in a garment?* **Who** *hath established all the ends of the earth?* **What** *is his name,* **and what is his son's name, if you can tell?**

There are actually six questions asked: five of them are known, but one of them is very perplexing to the rabbis, because without any hesitation they reject it, yet *HaShem* has placed it in His Word. The answer to the first four questions is G-d. The answer to the fifth question is *HaShem*. The sixth question is, *What is His* [*HaShem*'s] *son's name, if you can tell?* The answer is not Israel, who is called the first born son of *Elokim* in the Book of Exodus. The tone of the verse is that G-d's son's name was unknown to them. Could *HaShem* have a son? Isaiah is affirming this in Isaiah 9:6 [5] when he says *unto us* [Israel] *a son is given*. According to that text *HaShem* gave Him names such as W*onderful*

148

Counselor, the *mighty God*, the *everlasting Father* and the *Prince of Peace*. It is also alluded to in Genesis 3:15 with the **Seed** of the woman who consistently points to one individual who is a descendent of David, but who is also G-d, a son whom the virgin would bring forth (Isaiah 7:14). It is also strongly emphasized by the prophets from Moses to Nathan, to David, to Isaiah, to Jeremiah, to Micah, to Zechariah and to Malachi, *HaShem* from the very beginning has reviewed Himself as a plurality in one (*echad*), as Father, Son, and Spirit distinct from each other, yet equal.

Daniel 9:24-27

We want to look at one last passage in the Writings section of the *Tanakh*. But I have to warn you the rabbis have forbidden this passage because they are afraid of what will be seen. Rabbis for centuries have tried to discern the time of the coming of Messiah, the *Mashiach*. In fact over the centuries, because of the desire to return to Israel under the leadership of the Messiah, Jewish people have embraced 46 false messiahs. Due to this strong desire to return, they had failed to look at the Hebrew Scriptures to see what *HaShem* has laid out concerning His person, character, essence and the timing of His coming. So consequently they consistently ignored these passages because of who it points to. Let us read together Daniel 9:24-27:

> [24] **Seventy weeks** *are determined upon* **your people** *and upon* **your holy city,** *to finish the transgression, and to make an end of sins, and to make reconciliation for iniquity, and to bring in everlasting righteousness, and to seal up the vision and prophecy, and to anoint the most Holy.* [25] *Know therefore and understand, that* **from the going forth of the commandment to restore and to build**

149

Jerusalem unto the anointed [Messiah] the Prince shall be seven weeks, and three-score and two weeks: *the street shall be built again, and the wall, even in troublous times.* ²⁶ *And* **after threescore and two weeks shall the anointed** [Messiah] **be cut off,** *but not for himself: and the people of the prince that* **shall come shall destroy the city and the sanctuary;** *and the end thereof shall be with a flood, and unto the end of the war desolations are determined.* ²⁷ *And* **he shall confirm the covenant with many for one week:** *and in the midst of the week he shall cause the sacrifice and the oblation to cease, and for the overspreading of abominations he shall make it desolate, even until the consummation, and that determined shall be poured upon the desolate.*

There is so much covered in these four verses that I cannot possible cover it all. So I will be making several summary statements. In verse 24, the message to Daniel was that 70 sevens of weeks or 490 years[50] will be determined upon Israel and Jerusalem to accomplish six things as seen in verse 24. The first three deal with putting an end to sin and the last three deal with bringing in righteousness. This righteousness will come through the Righteous Branch (Jeremiah 23:5-6).

There are three types of offences against G-d mentioned in the first section on putting an end to sin: transgression, sin and iniquity. These are three descriptive words:

---

[50] See Leviticus 26:32-35; Jeremiah 25:8-12; 29:10; 2 Chronicles 36:21; Daniel 9:1-2, 24-27. Also notice Daniel's prayer of confession on behalf of the nation of Israel in verses 3-19.

- The **transgression** is singular, and means rebellion, one particular rebellion – Leviticus 26:40; Hosea 5:15; Zechariah 11:12-13; Psalm 22:14-18.

- **Sin** is missing the mark, the mark would be the holiness of *HaShem*, and man misses it – Leviticus 26:24, 28, 41; Deuteronomy 29:25-28; Isaiah 59:2-13; 64:6; Jeremiah 17:9.

- **Iniquity**, and the making of atonement for iniquity; iniquity carries the meaning of inward sin – Isaiah 1:2-18.

So the 70 sevens of years are to deal with the transgression, sin and iniquity, and when Israel embraces *Yeshua* the Messiah He will bring in the following three things that pertain to righteousness:

- Everlasting Righteousness because He is Righteousness – Jeremiah 23:5-6

- He will seal up the need for visions and prophecy for He, *HaShem*, is present; for the person who spoke to the prophets will be present in Jerusalem sitting on the throne of David.

- He will anoint the most Holy, which is the Millennial Temple – Ezekiel 40-48.

After setting up the framework of the 70 sevens of years, he proceeds to give the timing of those events. Daniel 9:25 states that from the going forth to restore and to rebuild Jerusalem it will be 69 sevens of years [Sabbatical years] or 483 years. The starting point of those weeks is in 444 BCE when Nehemiah received the commission from the king of Persia (read Nehemiah chapters 1-2) to restore and rebuild the wall and gates of Jerusalem. The end of 69 sevens, or 483 years is 30 CE.

Verse 26 states that the Messiah, the *anointed* one, will be *cut off*, which is a word for *execution*, at the end of those 483 years, which again is 30 CE. The prince who destroyed *the city and the sanctuary* in 70 CE was General Titus from Rome. That verse places the first coming of the Messiah or *Mashiach*, the *anointed* of *HaShem*, in the first half of the first century CE. To be precise, He was *cut off* in 30 CE. There is only one candidate that fulfills that timetable, and His name is *Yeshua* (Jesus) of Nazareth. Now look back at His credentials from Moses and the prophets:

- He must have a unique birth—**Seed** of the woman— Genesis 3:15;

- He will be a son of Abraham—the promised **Seed**— Genesis 22:18;

- He will be of the royal line, a son of Judah—the **King**—Genesis 49:10;

- He is the Angel bearing the Name of *HaShem* in Him—Exodus 23:20-23;

- He proceeds from Jacob—**King** and Star—Numbers 24:17;

- He will be a **Prophet**—like Moses —Deuteronomy 18:15-19; Numbers 12:5-8;

- He will be a son of David, from David's sons— I Chronicles 17:11;

- He must be Virgin born—Isaiah 7:14;

- He will be called Immanuel—Isaiah 8:8, 10;

- He would be G-d's own son – "Unto us a son is born," (Isaiah 9:6-7 [5-6[) then *HaShem* gave Him names that only apply to Himself—Jeremiah 23:5-6;

- The House of David will be in ruins—Isaiah 11:1; Amos 9:11;

152

- A forerunner will come before Him—Isaiah 40:3; Malachi 3:1;

- He is the Sent One—Isaiah 48:12-16;[51]

- He is the Creator—Isaiah 48:12-16; Zechariah 12:1, 10;[52]

- He will restore Jacob as the servant of *HaShem*—Isaiah 49:5;

- He will be scourged and beaten—Isaiah 50:1-6;

- He is the Suffering Servant—Isaiah 53;

- He is the Angel of His face—Isaiah 63:9;

- He will be the King of Righteousness meaning that Righteousness is His character, He is G-d as well as man—Jeremiah 23:5-6;

- He will be born in Bethlehem—Micah 5:2[1];

- He will be betrayed for 30 pieces of silver—Zechariah 11:12-13;

- He will be pierced with a sword; thrust through—Zechariah 12:10;

- He will be the G-d/man who is equal to *HaShem*—Zechariah 13:7;

- He will be the Messenger of the Covenant—Malachi 3:1;

- He is the Son of G-d—Psalm 2;

- He will die but not see corruption—Psalm 16;

- He will be resurrected—Psalm 16:10;

- He will die a horrible death on a Roman cross—Psalm 22;

---

[51] See the Gospel of John in chapter 5:37.
[52] See the Epistle to the Colossians in chapter 1:15-18.

- He is at the right hand of *HaShem* showing equality with *HaShem*—Psalm 80:17 [18];

- He is David's Lord and a priest after Melchizedek—Psalm 110:4;

- G-d asked for the name of His son—Proverbs 30:4;

- He came at the prescribed time—Daniel 9:24-27.

Let me give several other summary points that were not discussed:

- He is the Arm of *HaShem* — Isaiah 40:10-11; 48:14; 51:5, 9; 52:10; 53:1; 59:16; 62:8; 63:5, 12.

- He is the Covenant—Isaiah 42:6; 49:8; Jeremiah 31:31-34 [30-33]; Malachi 3:1.[53]

- He is the Rock—Deuteronomy 32:4, 15, 18, 30-31, 37; 1 Samuel 2:2; 2 Samuel 22:1-2; 32; 23:1-3; Psalms 18:1-2; 28:1; 31:2-3; 61:2 [3]; 89:26 [27].[54]

- He is the Word—Genesis 15:1, 4; Psalm 33:6.[55]

- He is the Shepherd of Israel—Zechariah 11:4-14; 13:7.[56]

- He is the Branch—Jeremiah 23:5-6; Zechariah 3:8; 6:12-13.

There are too many similarities between *Yeshua* the first-century rabbi and the prophesied Messiah to cast aside as simply coincidence. The prophecies are too precise and detailed to dismiss, yet for 2000 years that is exactly what

---

[53] Gospel of Matthew in the New Testament: Matthew 26:28

[54] Gospel of Matthew in the New Testament: Matthew 16:16

[55] Gospel of John in the New Testament: John 1:1-3, and Revelation 19:11-15.

[56] Gospel of John in the New Testament: John 10:11

rabbinic Judaism has done. You have been misled; from *HaShem*'s perspective it becomes increasingly clear why He has been silent to His first-born and why Jewish people have been eclipsed from G-d. The Hebrew Scriptures confirm that the Second Person of *Elokim* became flesh and was called *Yeshua*, the Hebrew word for Salvation [*Yeshuah*], then as a man He claimed to be G-d, the G-d/man promised in Genesis 3:15 (Isaiah 9:6-7 [5-6]). He began tearing down the "fence" of the Oral Law which was supplanting the Written Law of *HaShem*. Yes, the so called christian church has horribly persecuted you and your fathers because they did not follow the words of *Yeshua* and the Apostles. The church from the 4th century onwards corrupted themselves beyond belief. Most of the world today that calls itself christian are not followers of the words and teachings of *Yeshua* and the Apostles but have apostatized. They have a thin veneer of christianity over their unbiblical religion.

2 Chronicles 36

After all this, how do the Writings section end on this subject? In 2 Chronicles 36:21-23 it states:

> *21 To fulfill the word of the LORD by the mouth of Jeremiah, until the land had enjoyed her Sabbaths:* **for as long as she lay desolate she kept Sabbath, to fulfill 70 years.** *22 Now in the first year* **of Cyrus king of Persia,** *that the word of the LORD by* **the mouth of Jeremiah** *might be accomplished, the LORD stirred up the spirit of Cyrus king of Persia, that he made a proclamation throughout all his kingdom, and put it also in writing, saying,* *23* **Thus saith** [says] **Cyrus king of Persia,** *All the kingdoms of the earth hath the LORD God of heaven given me; and he hath charged me to build him an house in*

Jerusalem, which is in Judah. Who is there among you of all his people? The LORD his God be with him, and let him go up.

The end of Chronicles speaks to the return of Israel under Cyrus the King of Persia in 536 BCE. But also notice that it ties together the 70 years of captivity with Daniel, and in particular Daniel 9:24-27. So whether it is the Law, Prophets or the Writings, they all end their sections of the *Tanakh* with the fact that the *Mashiach* [Messiah] has not yet come, and each one gives a different aspect as to how to identify Him:

- Law—Like unto Moses;

- Prophets—Elijah will come first;

- Writings—Daniel gives a time table.

The seams between the divisions of the *Tanakh* also focus on the fact that until the *Mashiach* [Messiah] — the **Seed** of the woman — comes, Israel is to meditate on the Written Law of *HaShem*:

- Joshua 1:8;

- Psalm 1.

How many people, whether they be Jew are Gentile, meditate on the Word of *HaShem*? I would say very few. Consequently people do not know the heart or the Word of **HaShem** and therefore do not walk uprightly before *HaShem*.

The *Tanakh* is a marvelous book, with connections and interconnections throughout its pages as *HaShem* reveals Himself to Israel as a plurality in one (*echad*). The *Tanakh* prepared the way for the incarnation of *HaShem* Himself to be born and fulfill the promises of *HaShem* given to Moses

156

and the Prophets, so that we might recognize Him. If the words of the Prophets are true, and Jesus has fulfilled those words, then in His eternal state He is a member of the plurality of *Elokim*. What does that say about the teachings of rabbinic Judaism? What does that say about the reason for the eclipse of G-d?

If you are moved and your mind has been engaged by these Scriptures, consider buying a *Tanakh* and a New Testament and begin to read the words of *HaShem* for yourself. Find the *Elokim* [G-d] of your fathers, Abraham, Isaac and Jacob, and He will lead you to the Seed, the King and the Prophet.

Amos has described the eclipse of G-d from his people. What Amos said to Israel is relevant to this present day. Look at *HaShem*'s words through the prophet Amos:

> *A time is coming – declares my LORD God – when I will send a famine upon the land: not a hunger for bread or a thirst for water, but for hearing the words of the LORD. Men shall wander from sea to sea and from north to east to seek the word of the LORD, but they shall not find it.* (Amos 8:11-12)

> *And if they go into captivity before their enemies, there I will command the sword to slay them. I will fix My eye on them for evil and not for good.* (Amos 9:4)

> *Behold, the Lord God has His eye upon the sinful kingdom: I will wipe it off the face of the earth! But I will not wholly wipe out the House of Jacob – declares the LORD. For I will give the order and shake the House of Israel – through all the nations – as one shakes [sand] in a sieve, and not a pebble falls to the ground. All the sinners of My people shall perish by the sword,*

157

who boast, "Never shall the evil overtake us or come near us." (Amos 9:8-10) (Jewish Study Bible/JPS)

When Israel confesses its sin and offense to *HaShem* and embraces *Yeshua* as their Messiah and G-d, look at the promises given to Israel, the Jewish Hope in Amos 9:11-15:

[11] In that day will I raise up the tabernacle of David that is fallen, and close up the breaches thereof; and I will raise up his ruins, and I will build it as in the days of old:
[12] That they may possess the remnant of Edom, and of all the nations, that are called by my name, saith the LORD that doeth this.
[13] Behold, the days come, saith the LORD, that the plowman shall overtake the reaper, and the treader of grapes him that soweth seed; and the mountains shall drop sweet wine, and all the hills shall melt.
[14] And I will bring back the captivity of my people of Israel, and they shall build the waste cities, and inhabit them; and they shall plant vineyards, and drink the wine thereof; they shall also make gardens, and eat the fruit of them.
[15] And I will plant them upon their land, and they shall no more be pulled up out of their land which I have given them, saith the LORD thy God.

Chapter Ten:
The Branch

2 Samuel 23:1-5...God's Eternal Covenant with David

Previously, we have examined the themes of the Messiah as Seed, King, and Prophet, but in this chapter we will focus on another theme in the Scriptures: Messiah as the Branch. The prophets pick up this theme, which is based on the words of David, which restate G-d's everlasting covenant with him in 2 Samuel 23:1-5:

> *¹ Now these be the last words of David. David the son of Jesse said, and the man who was raised up on high, the anointed of the God of Jacob, and the sweet psalmist of Israel, said,*
> *² The Spirit of the Lord spoke by me, and his word was upon my tongue.*
> *³ The God of Israel said, the Rock of Israel spoke to me, He that ruleth over men must be just, ruling in the fear of God.*
> *⁴ And he shall be as the light of the morning, when the sun riseth, even a morning without clouds; as the tender grass springing out of the earth by clear shining after rain.*
> *⁵ Is not so my house with God? For he hath made with me an everlasting covenant, ordered in all*

things, and sure: yea, will he not cause to succeed
all my salvation, and all my desire, [to blossom].

David used the term *sprout* or blossom in
2 Samuel 23:5b, which states, *Will He not cause all my*
success and [my] *every desire to blossom* or to grow, sprout
[*tzemach*] (quoted from Jewish Study Bible).

Based on this reference by David, the prophets used the
word *branch* to reference the Messiah of Israel. It is
translated as *branch* or *sprout* and comes from the Hebrew
words *tzemach* and *netser*. The term *branch* becomes a very
technical term in referencing the *Mashiach*, the Messiah.
The question is, "What did David understand about this
word that means *to blossom, grow or to sprout?*"

In 2 Samuel 23, David in his old age is reflecting on the
everlasting covenant that *HaShem* made with him. He asks
this question rhetorically, *Will not God cause all my*
*salvation and all my desire to **sprout**?* Elsewhere, in
Psalm 132:17, a psalm of ascent, the psalmist is writing
concerning David. He states, *There will I make **the horn** of*
*David **to** bud* **[sprout]:** *I have ordained a lamp for mine*
anointed. The *horn* of David refers to his kingdom, his
dynasty, his throne; it will *sprout* and branch out. So after
David there was this understanding of the eternality of
David's throne. In Psalm 89, Ethan, who served under King
Solomon, also understood the eternality of the Davidic
Covenant. Let's see how the word *sprout* or *branch* is used
in reference to the Messiah several hundred years after the
time of David, and before the time of Jesus by several
hundred years.

Jeremiah 23:5-6 ...The Righteous Branch

⁵ Behold the days come, saith [says] *the LORD, that I will raise unto David a* **righteous sprout** [Branch], *and he shall reign as* **King** *and prosper and shall execute judgment and justice in the earth.* *⁶ In his days Judah shall be saved, and Israel shall dwell safely: and this is* **his name** *whereby he* **shall be called,** *THE LORD OUR RIGHTEOUSNESS.*

The prophet Jeremiah is the second prophet to use the term *Sprout* or *Branch* and makes it a technical word for the *Mashiach* [Messiah]. Zedekiah was king at the time of Jeremiah's prophecy, and he was the end of a long line of wicked kings, starting from Ahaz and Manasseh extending to all the sons and the grandson of Josiah who were wicked. Zedekiah was the actual last king of Judah whose name, ironically, meant "*Yahweh* is Righteousness."

Now this passage was written when Zedekiah was king, so Jeremiah will contrast the meaning of Zedekiah's name, who was wicked and unfaithful, to *a righteous Branch, who shall reign as a King*, and this king will be called *THE LORD OUR RIGHTEOUSNESS*. Because Zedekiah did not live up to his name, *HaShem will raise unto David a righteous Branch.* The contrast is clear; one was unrighteous in character, and the other, who is the righteous Branch, will be righteous by character. Notice, He will not *become* righteous, but will *be* righteousness.

The first book of the New Testament is the Gospel of Matthew, who focused on *Yeshua's* royal qualifications. Matthew's theme for his book is *Yeshua*, the Righteous Branch, King of the Jews. He wrote his book to show Jewish people that *Yeshua* was the promised one from Genesis to Chronicles, the one that Moses and the Prophets were referencing, the **Seed**, the Righteous **King** and the **Prophet**.

Zechariah 3:8 ... G-d's Servant the Branch

Hear now, O Joshua the high priest, you, and your fellows that sit before you: for they are men of distinction: for, behold, I will bring forth **my servant the BRANCH** *[of David].*

The prophet Zechariah is the third prophet to use the term *sprout* or *branch*, a technical word for the **Mashiach** [Messiah]. Zechariah prophesied during the post-exile period when 50,000 Jewish people returned from Babylon under the leadership of Zerubbabel. His prophecies fall in the late 6th century BCE. That's almost 100 years removed from Jeremiah and over 400 years removed from David.

Zechariah 3:8 is from a vision of Zechariah in which he is observing a court scene where Satan is raising a complaint to *the angel of the LORD* against Joshua the high priest. This is the same *angel of the LORD* that we meet in Genesis, the exodus from Egypt to Canaan, and in Judges. Let us look at the context of the vision in Zechariah 3:1-10:

¹ And he shewed [showed] me Joshua the high priest standing before the angel of the Lord, and Satan standing at his right hand to resist him.
² And the Lord said unto Satan, The Lord rebuke thee, O Satan; even the Lord that hath chosen Jerusalem rebuke thee: is not this a brand plucked out of the fire?
³ Now Joshua was clothed with filthy garments, and stood before the angel.
⁴ And he answered and spoke unto those that stood before him, saying, Take away the filthy garments

162

from him. And unto him he said, Behold, I have caused thine iniquity to pass from thee, and I will clothe thee with change of raiment.

⁵ And I said, Let them set a fair mitre upon his head. So they set a fair mitre upon his head, and clothed him with garments. And the angel of the Lord stood by.

⁶ And the angel of the Lord protested unto Joshua, saying,

⁷ Thus saith the Lord of hosts; If thou wilt walk in my ways, and if thou wilt keep my charge, then thou shalt also judge my house, and shalt also keep my courts, and I will give thee places to walk among these that stand by.

⁸ Hear now, O Joshua the high priest, thou, and thy fellows that sit before thee: for they are men wondered at: for, behold, I will bring forth **my servant the Branch.**

⁹ For behold the stone that I have laid before Joshua; upon one stone shall be seven eyes: behold, I will engrave the graving thereof, saith the Lord of hosts, and I will remove the iniquity of that land in one day.

¹⁰ In that day, saith the Lord of hosts, shall ye call every man his neighbour under the vine and under the fig tree.

Look at verse 3: *Now Joshua was clothed with filthy garments, and stood before the angel.* Notice that both Joshua and Satan are standing before *the angel of the LORD.* Also notice what the Angel does in verses 2 and 4. First He *rebukes* Satan and secondly He removes Joshua's *filthy garments* which symbolically stands for Joshua's and Israel's iniquity. Now one principle is clearly understood from the *Tanakh*: Only *HaShem* can rebuke Satan and only

HaShem can forgive and remove sins, and here *the angel of the LORD* is doing just that! He is Himself doing something that only G-d can do, forgive sins and rebuke Satan.

In verse 6-7 *the angel of the LORD* speaks as *HaShem* to Joshua, saying, if you obey *my ways*, and *keep my charge*, and *judge my house* and *my courts* you (Joshua) will be rewarded.

In verse 8 *the angel of the LORD* says that He [*HaShem*] *will bring forth my servant the Sprout [BRANCH] of David*. The Servant, the BRANCH is then directly connected to the *stone* that has *seven eyes* [verse 9] which *the angel of the LORD* has engraven, and then He speaks as *HaShem* again, saying that He, *the angel* [Messenger] *of the LORD will remove the iniquity of that land in one day*.

So we see in this passage that not only does *the angel of the LORD* remove sin from Joshua symbolically, but He will also remove iniquity from the Land in one day. *The angel of the LORD* is G-d, yet distinct from G-d; He is the Second Person of the plural unity of *Elokim*. Now that is still a future event to happen. Israel's iniquity still remains to this day. Look at the sin and vice that happens in places like Tel Aviv, Haifa, Tiberias and Jerusalem in Israel; and New York City, Chicago, Miami, and Los Angeles in the United States; Paris and London in Europe; or Buenos Aires, Argentina, or San Paulo, Brazil, in South America, to name only a few places. With the temple gone and no system to reunite Israel to G-d, the broken relationship with G-d has no remedy. Rabbinic Judaism offers no solution for reuniting G-d's people with *HaShem*. But because of the sin of Israel today, G-d has been silent, and the eclipse of G-d is present with the Jewish people today.

The good news is, this eclipse need not be, because the promised BRANCH would be sent, coming as a servant, the Servant of the *L-RD* that Isaiah spoke of in chapters 42, 49, 53, 61.

This good news is reiterated in the book of Mark, the second Gospel in the New Testament, which presents *Yeshua* as the Servant, the Branch. The New Testament was written by Jewish men, and they were knowledgeable about the prophecies of the *Tanakh.*

Zechariah 6:12 ... A Man Who Is the Branch with Two Crowns

For the second time Zechariah uses the technical term *Sprout* or *Branch*, but he introduces what appears to be a prohibited identity. In the context of Zechariah chapter 6, **Joshua** is mentioned again with the symbolic crowning of Joshua the high priest with not just one crown but **two crowns.** Zechariah is uniting two offices that in the *Tanakh* were forbidden to be held by a priest or the king. The record of King Uzziah is a clear breach of that command (II Chronicles 26:16-23). *Crowns* symbolizes a king *and* a priest, and a king under the Law cannot share his office with the priest or vice versa. In fact look with me at verses 12-13:

> *¹² And speak unto him, saying, Thus speaketh* **the LORD of hosts, saying, Behold the man whose name is the Sprout** [Branch]; *and he shall grow up out of his place, and* **he shall build the temple** *of the LORD:* *¹³ Even* **he shall build the temple** *of the LORD; and* **he shall bear the glory,** *and shall* **sit and rule upon his throne;** *and* **he shall be a priest upon his throne**; *and the counsel of peace shall be between them both.*

Here *HaShem* is distinctly saying that *the man*, one particular man whose name is the *Sprout* or *Branch*, is the *Mashiach* [Messiah]. What happens is that *the man whose name is the BRANCH* will build the Millennial Temple. He will bear the glory of *whom* in the Temple? He will bear the glory of *HaShem*. *The Mashiach* will sit on the throne as priest and king; under the Law that is not even a possibility. (However this priest will not be a Levitical priest but a priest after a different order, the order of Melchizedek, as prophesized in Psalm 110:1-4.[57]) Yet Zechariah reveals the *Branch* to be *the man* who is the Messiah, bearing the glory of *HaShem*.

The book of Luke, the third Gospel in the New Testament, presents the theme of *Yeshua* as *the man*, the Branch, the perfect Man.

Yahweh's Branch ... Isaiah 4:2; 11:1

The first prophet to use the technical term *Sprout* or *Branch* was Isaiah, and he used it twice, once each in Isaiah 4:2 and 11:1. These are the verses:

> [4:2] **In that day** *shall the* **branch of the LORD** *be beautiful and glorious, and the fruit of the earth shall be excellent and comely for them that are escaped of Israel.*

> [11:1] *And there shall come forth a rod out of the stem of Jesse, and* **a Branch shall grow out of his roots.** *And the spirit of the LORD shall rest upon him, ...*

The term *in that day* in Isaiah 4:2 is a reference to the time just before the Messiah comes and establishes the

---

[57] See New Testament book of Hebrew: Hebrews 7:1-28.

Kingdom, fulfilling all of the covenants: Abrahamic, Land, Davidic and New Covenants. Isaiah is drawing from David's and Ethan's statements (Psalm 89) and applies the term *branch* to *Yahweh* or *HaShem*. Here Isaiah states that the Branch is the *branch of the LORD*, the *Branch* of *HaShem, and he is emphasizing deity.*

Isaiah 4:2 presents the *Branch* as *HaShem*, the Branch that is divine; Isaiah 11:1 presents the humanity of the *Branch*.[58] That is very difficult to understand, but that is what Isaiah presents to the reader. Messiah will come in insignificance as from Jesse; He will not come in royal pomp. How can it be that He is divine, but also of humble origins?

Isaiah presents the Branch as both divine and human, and that is the theme of the book of John, which is the fourth Gospel in the New Testament. John presents *Yeshua* as the G-d/man combining both aspects of Isaiah 4:2 and 11:1. Just as the prophets focus on the four aspects of the Branch, each of the four Gospel writers pick up one of those four themes in presenting *Yeshua* as the Jewish Messiah.

Let us review what Jeremiah, Zechariah and Isaiah have already said about the Sprout, or Branch, the *Mashiach* (Messiah):

• Jeremiah 23: *Mashiach* will be the Righteous Branch for he embodies Righteousness, for His name is *THE LORD OUR RIGTHEOUSNESS*. Notice as well the Righteous Branch is a man who is raised up unto David. He will be the King of the Jews.

---

[58] Please see the New Testament Gospel of Luke chapter 4:16-21.

- Zechariah 3: Jeremiah presents the "King of Righteousness" facet of character of the Branch; here Zechariah presents Him as *"my Servant the Branch."* Zechariah is presenting Him as a man (the Righteous King) who will *"remove the iniquity of the land in one day."* Here is a man who will remove the iniquity of Israel, which only *HaShem* can do; He is the Servant, the Branch.

- Zechariah 6: Again Zechariah not only presents the *Mashiach* (Messiah) as a *servant* who will also be the Righteous King, but now he presents the *Branch*, the *Mashiach*, as the man *whose name is the Branch*. We have Zechariah presenting the human side of the *Mashiach*, with Jeremiah presenting His divine side as one who embodies Righteousness as the King. This man will be the Righteous and perfect Man, the Branch.

- Isaiah 4 and 11: Isaiah emphasizes both the deity of the Branch and the humanity of the Branch in these contrasting passages. This is a very hard concept for all Jewish people to believe, but these are the words of Isaiah the prophet of G-d.

In summary, the prophets declare that the Branch will be the Righteous Branch (*HaShem*), the King (a man), G-d's Servant the Branch (bringing reconciliation), a Man with two crowns (a human priest who rules, bearing *HaShem's* glory), and lastly, the Branch who is both divine and human (G-d's greatness manifested in the humble form of a man).

Chapter Eleven:
The Word of the *L-RD*

In chapter three we looked at the plural usage of the different names of G-d, plus pronouns and plural descriptions of G-d. This is in opposition to rabbinic Judaism that teaches absolute oneness. Yet there are an abundance of references in the *Tanakh* that point to a plurality in oneness, just like you are a plurality in one: body, soul and spirit. These references simply cannot be ignored or explained away. In this chapter we want to look at another descriptive term for *HaShem*: the Word of *HaShem*. The rabbis of the first century attributed several things to the Word (the *Memra*) of the *L-RD* (*HaShem*) which we want to briefly review.

The Word [Memra] - Distinct Yet Equal

First, we looked at the passages that show the *angel of the LORD* or *HaShem* equal to and yet distinct from *Elokim*.[59] Now there is another name for the Second Person of *Elokim*, the *Word of the LORD*, or the Word of *HaShem*. The rabbis of the past referred to Him as the *Memra*, Aramaic for "word." This distinction was seen in Genesis 15:1, 4 where the *word* was the maker of the Abrahamic Covenant (Judges 2:1) and is identified as *the word of the LORD, HaShem*, the *Memra*. The sages of old saw the distinction between *HaShem* and the Word of

---

[59] Gospel of John chapter 1:1-2

HaShem, the *Memra*; but they did not go far with it. However, they did see it.

The Word [*Memra*] - Agent of Creation

Secondly the rabbis saw that the Word of *HaShem*, the *Memra*, was the agent of Creation, a person, for Psalm 33:6 states the following:

> *By the word of the LORD were the heavens made; and all the host of them* **by the breath of his mouth**.

The psalmist is attributing personhood to the Word, the *Memra,* as a distinct person within the plurality of *Elokim*. It is also seen that the second person of *Elokim* was the creator in Isaiah 48:12-16, Zechariah 12:1, 10 and a plural to *Elokim* in Ecclesiastes 12:1.[60]

The Word [*Memra*] – Agent of Salvation

Thirdly, in Hosea 1:7 he attributes personhood to *the Word of the LORD* [*HaShem*] who provides salvation, for He states in verses 1 and 2 that *the Word of the LORD* [*HaShem*] is speaking, and He records what He says in verse 7:

> **But I will** *have mercy upon the house of Judah, and* **will save them by the** *LORD* **their God** [*Elokim*], *and will not save them by bow, nor by sword, nor by battle, by horse, nor by horsemen.*

---

[60] The New Testament Gospel of John in 1:1-3, 10 equates the Word with Messiah *Yeshua*.

Here Hosea 1:7 makes the Word of *HaShem*, the *Memra*, as the agent of Salvation.[61]

The Word [Memra] – Agent Whereby HaShem Revealed Himself

Fourthly, we also see the Word of *HaShem*; the *Memra* is the agent whereby *HaShem* revealed Himself to mankind.[62] Example: In Genesis 15, *HaShem* confirms the Abrahamic Covenant where *He* makes an eternal commitment with Abraham and to you as his descendants. But here we have a new name for *Elokim*, and He is acting independently and yet in harmony with *Elokim* as the Word of *HaShem*, the *Memra*. In verse one it states:

> *After these things* **the word of the LORD came unto Abram** *in a vision, saying, fear not, Abram: I am thy shield and your exceeding great reward.*

The same individual is speaking again in verse 4. Here it is not *HaShem*, *Elokim* or *Adhonai* that is speaking but *the Word of the LORD [HaShem]*, the *Memra*. *The Word of the LORD [HaShem]* makes the covenant with Abraham by walking between the cut animals [as the *Shechinah*] and not letting Abraham participate except to watch. This was a very serious blood covenant in ancient times between two parties. *The Word of the LORD [HaShem]* confirmed the covenant with Himself. Later in Judges 2:1 in the Prophets section of the *Tanakh*, we saw that it was *the angel of the LORD* that took Israel from Egypt to the Promised Land, and He states that He made that covenant. Yet rabbinic Judaism does not want to see this because it means a plurality in *Elokim* or *HaShem* which are used interchangeably through

---

[61] See the New Testament Gospel of John in chapter 1:12.
[62] See the New Testament Gospel of John in chapter 1:14.

171

the *Tanakh*. That being the case with all the other plural references in the *Tanakh*, opens the door that perhaps *Yeshua* was correct when He said, *I and the Father are one*,[63] or *if you have seen me, you have seen the Father*.[64] So here again is a reference to plurality in *Elokim*, the *Memra*, yet one. He is not divisible, He is indivisible; He is one (*echad*). This is not the only passage like that.

In 1 Samuel 3 you have the account of Samuel being raised by Eli the high priest and of *HaShem* speaking to him. Verse 7 makes *the Word of the LORD*, the *Memra* equal to and yet as distinct from *HaShem*. In verse 21 the following is stated:

> *And the* **LORD** **appeared** *again in Shiloh: for the* **LORD** **revealed Himself** *to Samuel in Shiloh* **by the** **Word of the** **LORD**.

HaShem appeared; this is the word for physical manifestation as in Genesis 12:7 and 17:1 where *HaShem appeared* to Abraham. According to 1 Samuel 3:21, *HaShem appeared* as *the word of the LORD*, or the *Memra* as a plurality in one [*echad*]. The Word of *HaShem*, the *Memra*, the Angel of *HaShem*, the Captain of the host of *HaShem*, the *Shechinah* glory or presence of *HaShem*, all show clearly the plurality of *Elokim* and *HaShem*. The Word of *HaShem*, the *Memra*, is one [*echad*] and yet distinct, a plurality as the Second Person of *Elokim* who revealed the Father to your fathers.

---

[63] See the New Testament Gospel of John in chapter 10:30.
[64] See the New Testament Gospel of John in chapter 14:9.

The Word [Memra] – Agent of Revelation

Fifthly, we also observe that it was *the word of LORD*, *HaShem*, the *Memra* that revealed the Father's will to Moses and the prophets. He was the agent of revelation who spoke to Abraham, Samuel, Nathan, Solomon, Elijah, Isaiah, Jeremiah, Ezekiel, Hosea, Joel, Jonah, Micah, Zephaniah, Zechariah and Malachi, just to name a few.[65]

The Word [Memra] – Agent Signing the Covenants

Lastly, *the word of LORD*, *HaShem* was the agent signing the covenants. We saw that the Word of *HaShem* gave the Abrahamic and Davidic Covenants. Yet *Yeshua*, at His last Passover with His disciples before His illegal trials and then crucifixion, took the third cup after the Passover meal, the cup of Redemption, and said that with His blood He would inaugurate the New Covenant spoken of by *HaShem* to Jeremiah 31:31-34 [30-33] (Isaiah 42:6). This is the circumcision of the heart spoken of by Moses (Deuteronomy 10:16; 30:6), Ezekiel (36:22-28) and Jeremiah (4:4; 9:25-26) as the answer to the rebellious heart of Israel.

Also observe Isaiah 42:6 where *HaShem* is speaking to the Servant of the *L-RD* who is the Messiah, as a Covenant for Israel and a light to the Gentiles.

> *I the LORD have called you in righteousness, and will hold thine hand, and will keep you, and give you for a covenant of the people, for a light of the nations* [Gentiles].

---

[65] See the New Testament Gospel of John in chapter 1:18.

Compare this verse from Isaiah with *Yeshua*'s use of the third cup at the Passover meal, the cup of Redemption, where He initiates or inaugurates the *New Covenant* of Jeremiah 31:31-34 [30-33] with His blood.[66]

We have seen that the *Tanakh* speaks of G-d as a plurality in unity (*echad*), whether it is the *angel of the LORD*, the *L-RD*, the Shechinah, the Creator, the Branch or the Word [*Memra*] of the *L-RD*. He has been presenting His oneness in plurality to Israel. The Word or *Memra* is also presented in a multi-faceted way, yet as one, as it relates to the six things that ancient rabbis saw and spoke of. There are too many incidents for this to be an accident within the pages of the *Tanakh*. The G-d of Israel purposely revealed Himself to Israel as a plurality in one (*echad*), but today as in the day of *Yeshua* it has become a very sensitive issue within Judaism. However, when the words of the Author of Scripture are studied, the reader begins to understand the person and heart of *HaShem* which over time has become eclipsed from His people Israel.

---

[66] See these New Testament Gospel passages: Luke 22:20; Mark 14:23-25; Matthew 26:26-29.

Chapter Twelve:
How Could *Yeshua* be the Messiah?

Why is it that Judaism and Christianity have never really gotten along? The christianity that your forefathers saw largely was a corrupted, compromised, criminal and apostate organization that directed its misguided zeal at your fathers for the death of *Yeshua* (Jesus). Spiritually behind the scenes was Satan using all his influence to build anti-Semitism even as he tried to work through evil Haman during the time of Queen Esther. The church after 325 CE compromised its faith and began to become, in many instances, a reprobate organization. Your fathers know all too well the result of that now as history stands. The Holocaust was the climactic result of all that heresy of the past on the part of so-called christians. Yet even out of the ashes of the Holocaust, *HaShem* was working through the Holocaust to cause the nations of the world to be sympathetic in the giving of rebirth to the Nation of Israel in 1948.

Does the great injustice of persecution justify throwing out the New Testament? The New Testament is not invalid because passages were taken out of context and used against the Jewish people. Furthermore, the New Testament does not teach idolatry. Practices like that came from the corruption of the Roman Catholic Church and other

Orthodox churches and is not from the New Testament. Anti-Semitism is not taught in the New Testament but it began coming into the church 300 years after the books of the New Testament were written. The New Testament does not in any way permit anti-Jewish teaching any more than the *Tanakh* does. The key is to interpret it literally and not take verses out of context or spiritualize the New Testament text to fit biases that have been passed on to us.

What Caused the Split?

If I may, let me paint a verbal picture for you as to why there is a division between real New Testament Faith and Judaism. Let me give several points.

Brokenness

- *HaShem* communicated Himself to your fathers and gave them a law to obey.

- However, Israel in rebellion to *HaShem* chose on a consistent basis to break the Law of Moses and worship pagan gods.

- *HaShem* followed through with the cursings (Deuteronomy 28:15-69) and finally by sending your fathers into the very center of idolatry, the Babylonian Empire. Israel learned her lesson well and forsook the worship of pagan gods, but they never really returned to *HaShem* with all their heart, soul, and might.

Defensiveness

Upon returning from captivity your fathers said that was not a good experience and we do not want to repeat it again. So we will make sure that we never again worship pagan gods. Their focus was on the oneness of *HaShem*, and rightfully so. That presented to them a problem because as the scribes studied the *Tanakh* they saw some of the same plural references that I have shown in this book. They wrestled with them, but because of their strong focus on the oneness of *HaShem*, they choose absolute oneness [*yachid*] thus laying aside what *HaShem* was saying. They said, "This cannot be so; *HaShem* is not plural, He is one [*yachid*]. There must be another answer." They did not grasp the fact that *HaShem* did present Himself as one, but as a one in unity, meaning there is a plurality of persons in that unity of one [*echad*].

Now you know the difference between those two Hebrew words, *echad* and *yachid*. Judaism explained away what *HaShem* had said about Himself because they never again wanted to be guilty of worshipping idols. So they forged ahead with the idea of the absolute oneness [*yachid*] of *HaShem* rather than accepting the plurality in oneness [*echad*].

A Stumbling Stone

Then came Jesus of Nazareth who claimed that He and the Father were one [*echad*], and that He was part of the plural unity of *Elokim* who came as the Messiah prophesied by Moses and the prophets in the *Tanakh*, to reveal the Father in person to Israel. The Pharisees and Sadducees could not accept this because of their focus on absolute oneness [*yachid*] instead of being able to see what the *Tanakh* presented: a plurality in one [*echad*].

Jesus also attacked the Oral Law as man-made rules and regulations and as not coming from Sinai. For this the Pharisees despised Him. The Pharisees then attributed everything that *Yeshua* did to the power of the devil.[67] From that point on they looked for an opportunity to have Him removed or killed. So-called christians centuries later picked that up and called you "Christ-killers." In their spiritual stupidity they failed to see that the prophets said the Messiah would come and suffer and die for the sins of both Jew and Gentile. So-called christians pointed the finger at Jewish people, and yet the church was just as rebellious and disobedient to the teachings of Jesus and the Apostles as Israel was in their disobedience to Moses and the prophets. Human sinful nature is the same whether one is Jewish or Gentile. We are all sinners by nature and practice, often with our fists raised to the heavens telling *HaShem* that we are going to do it our way (Isaiah 53:6), and to just get out of our lives, and He did. Then we wonder why He is silent! Today this is true of Jewish people as it is true among so-called christians.

Theological Interpretation Regarding the Messiah

One Appearance or Two?

New Testament believers teach that according to the *Tanakh* one Messiah will make two appearances, **first** as the suffering Messiah who will die for the sins of the world so that the relationship between a holy G-d and sinful man can be restored. **Secondly**, the Messiah will return as the ruling King who will establish the Messianic Kingdom and fulfill all the promises that He made to Abraham, David and Israel as is recorded in the Hebrew Scriptures. However, on this issue rabbinic Judaism completely disagrees. Yet religious orthodox Jewish people believe in a personal coming

---

[67] See the New Testament Gospel of Matthew in chapter 12:22-45.

messiah; however, they believe in two *human* messiahs whom they call Messiah ben Joseph who will suffer and die and Messiah ben David who will come and reign.

One Messiah or Two?

What is interesting is that we both see the Messiah making two appearances but disagree on the identity and character of the Messiah. New Testament believers say that the Messiah is *Yeshua*, G-d incarnate who will make two appearances. Rabbinic Judaism sees two individual human messiahs making two separate appearances. My Jewish friends tell me that secular Judaism as well as Reform and most of Conservative Judaism does not believe in a personal messiah at all. They just believe that it is up to them to make the world better. Let me ask a straightforward question in all honesty: Is it working for you?

So first there was a theological difference between Judaism and Christianity on the deity of *Yeshua*. Today both Judaism and Christianity call themselves monotheistic. Judaism, in not understanding the *Tanakh*, the Law and Prophets, calls true New Testament believers who believe in G-d the Father, G-d the Son and G-d the Spirit, *tri-theists*. They assert that true New Testament believers worship three gods and are thus idolaters. Then on the back of that came the anti-Semitic history of the church which made the wall between Jewish people and true New Testament believers almost insurmountable. So here we are today alienated from each other because of the ancient rabbis' refusal to see what *HaShem* had written and because of the blindness of christianity in hating the Jewish people and holding them responsible for the act of "killing G-d," if that were possible. Both groups actually stand guilty before a holy G-d who must judge both groups for their sins.

Chapter Thirteen:
How Can You Know Him
When He Comes?

Historically rabbis have rejected the claims of *Yeshua* being the promised Messiah of Israel, *first*, because He claimed to be G-d, and, *secondly*, because they focused only on one aspect of the coming of Messiah. They focused only on the Coming King instead of putting together the two comings of Messiah. In His first coming He came to die as a sacrifice for sin by shedding His blood before then coming a second time as the King, to fulfill the promised covenants. Sin that separates man from G-d must be dealt with first, from G-d's perspective. That was the first priority before the covenants could be fulfilled. I say all this because rabbinic Judaism had taught that the Messiah would come as the conquering King. Because *Yeshua* did not set up the Kingdom, to them He was not the Messiah. Here are four common objections to *Yeshua* as the Messiah sent by G-d:

First, rabbis say that He did not build the temple because Herod's Temple was still standing in 30 CE. Yet in Daniel 9:24-27, *HaShem* states that the Messiah will come and be *cut off* and *the city and the sanctuary* will be destroyed. It is Zechariah who speaks to *Mashiach* (Messiah) coming and building what will be the Millennial Temple (Zechariah 6:12; 1 Chronicles 17:12). Notice also Ezekiel chapters 40 through 48 as the Millennial Temple is described; it will be more glorious than Herod's Temple. Also the *Shechinah* that departed from Solomon's Temple (Ezekiel chapters 8 through 11) did not return to Zerubbabel's Temple or the refurbished Herod's Temple. His coming is still future.

Secondly, rabbis say that *Yeshua* did not re-gather the Jewish people from the Diaspora; therefore He is not the Messiah. In fact after 70 CE, the Diaspora was even greater. *First* of all *Yeshua* was not accepted as the *Mashiach*. *Secondly*, the re-gathering did not occur: Why? Did the New Covenant take full effect? Was Israel's heart circumcised (Deuteronomy 30:6; Jeremiah 31:31-34; Ezekiel 36:23-35; Isaiah 59:20-21; Romans 11:25-28)? Did salvation come to Israel in one single day like the prophets recorded in *HaShem*'s Word? No, so that the deliverance, redemption and salvation of Israel is still future as the prophets said, but days of trouble lay yet before you prior to His covenants being fulfilled. What is clear from Scripture is that the Messiah will not force His way into Israel's lives as King. Only when He is voluntarily accepted on Israel's part will He set up the Kingdom. So the Diaspora was magnified, not reversed, and it continues today. But the return in unbelief has begun (Ezekiel 37).

Thirdly, they say that *Yeshua* did not bring peace, which is absolutely correct. But the flip side of that is, how could He bring peace when the Jewish religious leadership in the first century CE rejected Him and that rejection was violent? Rabbinic Judaism will continue to say that the "Christian religion" was started by His followers who brought the sword. Again several hundred years later that did become a reality. But again the church apostatized and was no longer faithful to *Yeshua* and the Apostles' teachings. The historic church was NEVER to use the sword or control governments, but to love, which they largely failed with a capital F to do.

The rabbis say that all the miracles that *Yeshua* did He did by the power of the devil and not by the power of *HaShem*.[68] Even the *Talmud* does not deny that *Yeshua* ministered in the early part of the 1st century CE doing many miracles. But because of *Yeshua*'s claims of deity and His desire to dismantle the Oral Law, the religious leadership completely rejected His offer of the Kingdom, which involved putting their faith and trust in *Yeshua*, by believing in Him as the Prophet like Moses. At that point *Yeshua* withdrew the offer of the Kingdom, but will re-offer the Kingdom to a later, still-future generation. The miracles were His signature that He had the power resident in Him to bring in the Kingdom; but He was rejected. What of the 46 false messiahs that Israel followed that disillusioned the Jewish people? Did any of them raise the dead, cleanse lepers, give sight to the blind, heal the lame and crippled, walk on water, feed 5,000 with two loaves of bread and five fish or any other miracles which were so numerous the Pharisees could not deny them occurring? Instead of accepting who He was by His impressive resume—works and words—the Sanhedrin (Pharisees and Sadducees) asserted that the power behind *Yeshua* was Satan, and that created the unpardonable sin of Israel by *HaShem*. That kind of rejection happened two other times in Jewish biblical history, and physical judgment was the net result. Let me give you the two examples of rejection where *HaShem* said the sin was unpardonable and must be physically judged:

---

[68] By the way, as a side thought, they believed in a personal devil [Satan] whereas the rabbinic Judaism of today has created the evil inclination to replace him.

1. In the Books of Moses, the *Torah*, Numbers chapters 13 through 14, Israel stood at the entrance to the Promised Land, and the people rebelled against *HaShem* because they accepted the unbelieving report of 10 of the 12 spies. Think of it, after all the miracles and provisions that *HaShem* had done, Israel rejected Moses and *HaShem* and wanted to return to Egypt. What happened? The offer of entrance into the Promised Land was withdrawn, and for 38 years—until that generation over the age of 20 died—the Israelites wandered in the wilderness. A new generation came up and those who were under 20 at the time of Numbers 13-14 were re-offered the Land; they obeyed and entered the Land. The earlier rejection was called an unpardonable sin on Israel's part. Why did *HaShem* withdraw the entrance to the Land? It was because of rebellion and unbelief.

2. In 2 Kings 21-22; 2 Chronicles 33-34 and Jeremiah 15:4 King Manasseh does the same kind of rejection. Because of his wickedness and the corruption of the people of the Land, *HaShem* said to King Josiah, the grandson of Manasseh, that because of Israel's sin they would go into captivity and no amount of repentance would change His mind.

This also became a reality for the Jewish people with *Yeshua*. He was the promised *Mashiach* (Messiah), but Israel had to willingly accept Him and obey Him freely and voluntarily in order for him to be their Messiah. He would not force Himself upon them. They had to willingly believe Him, His Word and miracles and embrace Him before He would install the Kingdom, but Israel did not embrace Him.

Fourthly, another reason why Judaism has not accepted *Yeshua* is because *Yeshua* did not install the Kingdom;

therefore, He cannot be the Messiah. Yet while the rabbis say they freely acknowledge from the Hebrew text that there are two different descriptive passages concerning the suffering and reigning Messiah, they would not embrace Him. Compare what rabbinic Judaism says with what *HaShem* said:

Rabbinic	*HaShem*
Two Messiahs	One Messiah
Two Messiahs coming once each	One Messiah coming twice
Suffer and die	Suffer and die
Would be resurrected	Would be resurrected
Come and reign	Come and reign
Fades away for G-d reigns	He is the G-d/man son of David who reigns on the throne of David as G-d

So you have two differing descriptions: one from rabbinic Judaism and one from *HaShem*. The issue is, who is He? What is His identity? The first messiah the rabbis named Messiah ben Joseph, the one who will come and die. It is interesting that is exactly what happened to *Yeshua*, as part of G-d's plan revealed by *HaShem* through Moses, David, Isaiah and others. The second messiah they named Messiah ben David, the one who will reign. So they saw two separate messiahs, however, both completely human. Yet today they still reject *Yeshua* for not setting up the Kingdom the first time, but neither does the first rabbinic messiah set up the Kingdom. They rejected *Yeshua*'s claim, and as a result He suffered and died as Psalms 16 and 22 and Isaiah 52:13 through 53:12 claims. The Servant passage in Isaiah 53 spoke of His substitutionary sacrifice for the sins of Israel. So both first coming Messiahs die and are resurrected: the rabbinic messiah and *HaShem*'s Messiah. The rabbinic messiah will die in battle; *Yeshua* died because He was rejected and hated by His own. But he died as the perfect Lamb of G-d. Just as the lamb of old died in the place of the deserved sinner, so Messiah, the Lamb of G-d died in the sinner's place, for both Jew and Gentile. Consequently, because of the rejection, He rescinded the offer of the Kingdom. *Yeshua* made an interesting statement in Matthew 23:37-39:

> *37 O Jerusalem, Jerusalem, thou that killest the prophets, and stones them which* **are sent unto you, how often would I have gathered** *your children together, even as a hen gathereth her chickens under her wings, and you would not!* *38 Behold, your house is left unto you desolate.* *39* **For I say unto you, you shall not see me henceforth, till you shall say, Blessed is he that cometh in the name of the** ***LORD***.

Notice that *Yeshua* was speaking as the G-d of Abraham, Isaac and Jacob when He said "I." He did not say that it was the Father who wanted to gather Israel together whom Israel refused. According to His words it was He who sent the prophets that Israel stoned and killed; it was He who wanted to gather together and protect and provide for the children of Israel. Notice in verse 39 He states that which the rabbis say is a messianic salutation or greeting when the Messiah comes: *Blessed is he that cometh in the name of the LORD.*

The next time He comes it will be the second coming, but He will only come to Israel when they acknowledge Him for who He is and call for Him to return. *Yeshua* in His last public statement quoted above said, *you shall not see me henceforth, till you shall say, Blessed is He that cometh in the name of the LORD.* He is the Second Person of the plural unity of *Elokim*, of whom Moses and the prophets spoke. This Messianic salutation will have to be given before He will come and deliver Israel from the hands of the Satan empowering the anti-Christ. That salutation comes from Psalm 118:26, part of the *Hallel* Psalms often read at Passover. This greeting will be preceded by a prayer of repentance and confession (Isaiah 53) as to *the transgression* of Daniel 9:24 and *the iniquity* of Leviticus 26:40, which was the sin that Hosea in 5:15 spoke of that caused Him to return to His place.

How can we know Yeshua was the Messiah?

He did not set up the Kingdom in His first coming because of rejection. But if you read the Gospel accounts of *Yeshua*'s ministry you will discover that the miracles that He did before the nation of Israel were His signature. They were glimpses of His power, that if unleashed would bring in the Kingdom. Look at a brief summary of those miracles and remember the rabbis of the first century did not dispute His miracles, only the source of His miracles:

- He healed the lame (Matthew 15:30-31; 21:14; Luke 14:13);

- He opened the eyes of the blind (Matthew 9:27-34);

- He opened the eyes of one born blind (John 9:1-41);

- He healed people with disfigured limbs (Matthew 12:9-14; Mark 3:1-6; Luke 6:6-11);

- He cleansed lepers (Matthew 8:2-4; Mark 1:40-45; Luke 5:12-16; Luke 17:11-37);

- He healed the paralytic (Matthew 9:1-8; Mark 2:1-12; Luke 5:17-26);

- He healed the impotent man (John 5:1-47);

- He healed the deaf and dumb (Matthew 15:29-38; Mark 7:31-8:9);

- He healed the deaf and dumb and demon-possessed (Matthew 12:22-37; Mark 3:19-20);

- He healed the man with dropsy: edema-water retention in soft tissues of the body (Luke 14:1-6);

- He raised the dead (Luke 7:11-17);

- He raised from the dead Jairus' daughter (Matthew 9:18-26; Mark 5:21-43; Luke 8:40-46);

- He resurrected Lazarus from death (John 11:1-44);

- He healed the woman with the issue of blood (Matthew 9:18-28; Mark 5:21-43; Luke 8:40-56);

- He healed the woman who had infirmities for 18 years (Luke 13:10-21);

- He replaced the ear of the servant of the high priest that Peter had cut off (Luke 22:51);

- He fed 5,000 people at one sitting with five loaves and two fish (Matthew 14:13-21; Mark 6:30-44; Luke 9:10-17; John 6:1-13);

- He fed 4,000 people at one sitting with seven loaves (Matthew 15:29-38; Mark 7:31-8:9);

- He walked on the water (Matthew 14:24-33; Mark 6:47-52; John 6:16-21);

- He commanded the fish into Peter's nets once (Matthew 4:18-22; Mark 1:16-20; Luke 5:1-11); and again a second time (John 21);

- He calmed the storm on the Sea of Galilee (Matthew 8:18, 23-27; Mark 4:35-41; Luke 8:22-25);

- He sat on a colt that had never been ridden (Matthew 21:1-11, 14-17; Mark 11:1-11; Luke 19:29-44);

- He changed water into wine (John 2:1-11);

- He cast out demons: the Capernaum demoniac (Mark 1:21-28; Luke 4:31-37); the Gadarene demoniacs (Matthew 8:28-34; Mark 5:1-20; Luke 8:26-39); the demoniac boy (Matthew 17:14-20; Mark 9:14-29; Luke 9:37-43);

- He caused the fish that Peter caught to have a *shekel* in its mouth for Peter to pay the temple tax (Matthew 17:24-27);

- He healed the sick when He was not even physically present (John 4:46-54);

- He healed the Centurion's servant (Matthew 8:5-13; Luke 7:1-10).

Luke records *Yeshua's* testimony to John the Baptist (Immerser) as he sat in Herod's prison. John had sent two disciples to erase his own doubts about the Messiahship of *Yeshua*. In Luke 7:19-23 is recorded what *Yeshua* does and says to confirm His Messiahship to John the Baptist:

> [19] *And John calling unto him two of his disciples sent them to Jesus, saying, Art thou he that should come? or look we for another?* [20] *When the men were come unto him, they said, John Baptist hath sent us unto thee, saying, Art thou he that should come? or look*

we for another? ²¹ And in that same hour he cured many of their infirmities and plagues, and of evil spirits; and unto many that were blind he gave sight. ²² Then Jesus answering said unto them, Go your way, and tell John what things ye have seen and heard; how that the blind see, the lame walk, the lepers are cleansed, the deaf hear, the dead are raised, to the poor the gospel is preached. ²³ And blessed is he, whosoever shall not be offended in me.

Jesus is here referencing the prophets as to their message concerning what Messiah will do (Isaiah 35:4-6 [5-7]; 61:1). No person in the history of the world has ever been able to do such things. None of the 46 false messiahs that Israel followed could put these on their personal resume. He had the power resident in Him to establish the Kingdom, to remove the curse from the ground and nature (Genesis 4:1, 5:29; Isaiah 2:4; 11:6-8; 65:25). He had the power to remove the curse from the animal kingdom and to allow mankind to live for a millennium or 1000 years, which is just the beginning, for that will be followed by the Eternal Order. He will have the power to stop the aging process (Genesis 5:6-31), and sickness—that all resided in His being because of who He was.

EPILOGUE:
A Special Word to the Covenant People of Israel

As a true New Testament believer in Jesus who firmly believes that the Jewish people are the elect and chosen people of G-d, and as a Christian Zionist, I recognize that the topic of this book is rejected by rabbis and usually Jewish people in general. Without one bit of hesitation I believe Israel's best days are ahead. But before those days arrive some very dark, dreadful days will come. The Abrahamic Covenant that G-d made with your fathers Abraham, Isaac and Jacob is an eternal covenant. It is the kind of covenant that if G-d does not fulfill it for all faithful believing Jewish people, past, present and future, then G-d is not G-d and the Hebrew Bible as well as the New Testament are all worthless.

The whole picture of the Hebrew Scriptures and the New Testament is that G-d chose Israel to be His instrument to reveal Himself to the Gentiles. But Israel continually sinned against G-d, causing Him to bring His judgment upon the nation of Israel. However, the promise of G-d given by Him to the prophets through the centuries remains; His love will once again be poured out on you as a nation, and Israel will rule over the nations by the hand of Messiah from the throne of David. However, if you have studied the *Tanakh*, you understand that the *day of the LORD*, or *the time of Jacob's trouble* also known as the last days, will occur before the Kingdom is realized by Israel. This period of time has also been called the Tribulation, the time when the battle of Armageddon will occur. I believe the rabbis of the past referred to it as the "birth pangs of the Messiah." What I am about to ask you to read has to do with those days called "the birth pangs of the Messiah" that Israel will experience before they are redeemed by *HaShem*. For you as Jewish people it has been 2400 years since the last prophet spoke to Israel. For true New Testament believers it has been 1900 years since the John the Apostle recorded the final words in the book called "Revelation." I would like to lay out for you a very general process of events—a chronology of events—so that when they happen you will recognize them clearly and understand that the redemption of Israel is very near. These events as they are laid out may overlap or may have one event happening shortly before or after what I have written down. In other words, some of these events may occur very close together. I will simply go through them point by point.

Birth Pangs of Messiah

1. It is believed by many conservative New Testament believers and scholars that nation against nation and kingdom against kingdom was the *first* of the "birth pangs of Messiah" and began in 1914 with the beginning of World War I and ended at the end of World War II. History recognized WWI and WWII as the same war with a 20-year pause between conflicts (Matthew 24:5-8).

2. In 1948, as a result of the Holocaust, the *second* birth pang occurred which was the establishment of the State of Israel for the first time in 1878 years.

Ezekiel 37 states that Israel will return to the land in unbelief.

3. In 1967 the *third* birth pang occurred when Israel won the Six-Day War where they obtained the West Bank or the biblical territory called the *mountains of Israel* with full control of Jerusalem. Without the West Bank area in Israel's possession Ezekiel chapters 38 through 39 could not occur, for Gog and Magog will come upon the *mountains of Israel* as they attack Israel.

Apostasy and Disappearances

The christian church today is largely an apostate body; many members are not true believers in Messiah. Being Gentiles we are true New Testament believers not because we are born Christian or baptized into Church as a baby. That is NOT biblical Christianity. True genuine believers who have made a personal decision to embrace Jesus (*Yeshua*) as their Saviour and Lord are the true Church, known as the body of Christ (Messiah). We believe that Jesus will return and take all believers out of this world to be with Him in heaven (1 Thessalonians 4:13-18) **before the day of the *LORD*.**

So someday in your future you will receive world-wide news reports that true New Testament believers in Jesus have suddenly disappeared; it is called the Rapture, or the catching up of the true Church. The apostate church will remain to be judged by the coming *Day of the LORD. The Day of the LORD* to come is from the wrath of the Lamb (Revelation 6:16). At that point in time Israel will have lost its best and only friend. There is no biblical date or time given for the Rapture, but it is believed that this will happen before the seven-year period known as the 70th week of

Daniel, the Great Tribulation, *the time of Jacob's trouble* (Daniel 9:24-27; Revelation 4-19).

Imminent Unfulfilled Prophecies

The following events have not happened yet but will happen before the tribulation.

1. **A Regional Attack on Israel.** Before the day of the *L-RD,* Russia, Iran, Turkey and other northern Islamic confederate nations will attack Israel according to Ezekiel 38-39. That will also include several nations from Africa, Liberia, Sudan and Somalia. What Ezekiel describes in the text is that there will be no one who will come to Israel's aid, which means that the United States of America will not defend Israel. The reason for that is unknown. Ezekiel states that G-d will step in personally and not only defend Israel, but miraculously, supernaturally destroy Israel's enemies completely. This will result in two major changes: (1) It will cause a resurgence in Jewish people to return to their G-d, the G-d of Abraham, Isaac and Jacob, the G-d of Israel (Ezekiel 39:22). Jewish people will in effect say to themselves, "G-d did not die in the Holocaust!" (2) The nations that attack Israel will be predominately Moslem. It will shatter the Islamic world when they realize that Allah of Mohammed (Arabic word for G-d) did not fight for them but was completely impotent as the G-d of Israel destroys these Islamic countries along with Russia just as in ancient times. That will cause great disillusionment among Islamic peoples who will realize what they have been taught for centuries was not true and that the G-d of Israel, He is G-d alone and not

Mohammed's Allah (Ezekiel 39:21). Not only does *HaShem* destroy the armies but He also destroys parts of their countries. Ezekiel also states that there will be earthquakes in the land of Israel and Jerusalem itself. Will that be the method *HaShem* uses to destroy the Dome of the Rock and the al-aqsa mosque on the Temple Mount? With Islam shattered, Israel would be free to build in Jerusalem the third of four Temples, known as the Tribulation Temple, without concern of infuriating the Islamic countries.

2. **A Total Blackout.** According to the prophet Joel (2:10) there will be a worldwide blackout, meaning that there will be no light from the sun, moon or stars. This will be the first of five that will occur: one before the day of the *L-RD* and four during the day of the *L-RD*.

3. **Elijah's Return.** According to the prophet Malachi (4:5) the *L-RD* will send Elijah the prophet **before** *the day of the L-RD*.

4. **Jacob's Trouble**. Next the Tribulation period of seven years in duration will begin which is the 70th Week of Daniel found in Daniel 9:24-27. The period will begin with Israel signing a peace covenant with a world leader. Israel will sign a seven-year peace pact with a leader of Roman descent from the western nations to provide safety and security for Israel (Daniel 9:26-27; Matthew 24:15-31). As true New Testament believers understand it, this leader will be the anti-Christ, a person indwelt and empowered by Satan himself.

5. **Staggering Death Tolls.** This will begin the period known as the 70th week of Daniel recorded in Daniel 9:24-27. During this period worldwide destruction and loss of life will be staggering, for half the world's population will perish during this time (Revelation 4-19). The world's population stood at over 7,072,186,291 persons as of December 2012. The New Testament Book of Revelation states that one-half of the world population will die during the seven-year period called the 70th week of Daniel. Also, two-thirds of Jewish people in the world will die at the hands of the anti-Christ as Holocaust II unfolds. It will be a horrible time for those living on the earth.

6. **The Third Temple and the Two Witnesses**. Somewhere around the time of the signing of the covenant or at the destruction of Gog and Magog, Israel will begin and complete construction on their third Temple. The New Testament Book of Revelation also states that G-d will seal 144,000 Jews at that time who will recognize what is going on and that Jesus or *Yeshua* is indeed the Messiah of Israel (Revelation 7:1-8). They will become evangelists taking the Gospel of Messiah to the ends of the earth. Also at this time there will be two men who are simply called the *two witnesses* who will do their ministry in Jerusalem (Revelation 11:3-12; Zechariah 4:1-7). In the middle of the 70th week, after 3½ years, they will finally be killed by the anti-Christ and the whole world will rejoice at their death and give gifts to each other. Their bodies will lie in the streets of Jerusalem for 3½ days; and then they will come back to life, be resurrected, and ascend into heaven as the whole world beholds in fear.

7. **The Anti-Christ Claims Deity.** In the middle of the 70th week, when the leader, the anti-Christ of the western nations, comes to defend Israel, he will make his move to proclaim himself as god by setting himself up as god in the new temple just built in Jerusalem (Matthew 24:15; Daniel 9:27; 7:8).

8. **The Anti-Christ Attacks Israel.** Israel is told in Scripture to flee (Matthew 24:16-22; Revelation 11:2) for the anti-Christ will unleash his fury upon them in what could be called "Holocaust II." He will be bent on the complete destruction of every Jewish person in the world, and Zechariah 13:8-9 tells us that two-thirds of the Jewish population will be killed during that time but one-third will survive.

9. **The Remnant of Israel Flees to Safety.** It is believed that Israel will flee to Petra, in Hebrew known as *Bozrah*, in Jordan (Micah 2:12-13; Isaiah 34:1-8; 63:1-6; Habakkuk 3:3). The Jewish people will lose the Land one more time for 3½ years as they flee from the anti-Christ to G-d's prepared place of protection where He will miraculously provide for her, the remnant of Israel that survives the onslaught of the anti-Christ.

10. **The Anti-Christ Pursues the Remnant.** As the anti-Christ destroys Jerusalem and Israel, he will proceed in his goal to kill the remnant of Jewish people hiding in Petra (*Bozrah*).

11. **Messiah Is Summoned.** During this time the rabbis will be searching the Scriptures and will come to the reality that Jesus or *Yeshua* was indeed the Son of G-d, the Son of David, the Messiah; and they will call for His return (Psalm 80:17; Daniel 7:13-14;

Hosea 5:15-6:3; Matthew 23:37-39). Because of Israel's repentance, faith and confession of their sin to *HaShem* concerning *Yeshua* the Messiah (Isaiah 53:1-9), Israel will be saved (Isaiah 59:20-21; Romans 11:26-27) and the New Covenant will be fulfilled with Israel being circumcised in heart (Deuteronomy 30:6).

12. **Deliverance and Judgment**. Messiah will return and personally destroy the anti-Christ and all his armies as He fights His way from Petra back to Jerusalem (Zechariah 14:3-4). In the Valley of Jehoshaphat (Kidron Valley that parallels Jerusalem and the Mount of Olives), He will judge the nations for how they treated Israel (Matthew 25:31-46).

13. **A Geographic Upheaval in the Middle East.** According to the Books of Ezekiel and Revelation there will be a great topography change in Israel and in the whole world. In the center of Israel there will be a 50-square-mile mountain plateau which will be the highest mountain on the earth with the Millennial Temple (one mile square) and the New Jerusalem (10 miles square) with the remaining land for the inhabitants of Jerusalem and land for the Levites. Israel border's will be greatly enlarged with seven tribes located north of the millennial mountain of *HaShem* absorbing most of Lebanon and part of Syria, and five tribes located south of the millennial mountain of *HaShem*.

14. **Messiah's Reign and the Fourth Temple**. Within a matter of 75 days after the 70th week, *Yeshua* the Messiah will set up the Messianic Kingdom and rule and reign over the world from the throne of David in Jerusalem and establish righteousness and peace for

1,000 years. At that point in time in Jerusalem the fourth Temple will be built, as described in Ezekiel, chapters 40 through 48.

For your interest and further study I would like to recommend to you five books that deal with Israel, the Messiah and Israel's covenants and its prophetic future:

1. *Israelology: The Missing Link in Systematic Theology.* Written by Dr. Arnold G. Fruchtenbaum and published by Ariel Ministries in 1994 (revised), now located in San Antonio, TX. www.Ariel.org (ISBN: 0-914863-05-3)

2. *The Footsteps of Messiah: A Study of the Sequence of Prophetic Events.* Written by Dr. Arnold G. Fruchtenbaum, published by Ariel Ministries in 2003 (revised). *www.Ariel.org,* (ISBN: 0-914863-09-6). Also available in e-Book download.

3. *Discovering the Mystery of the Unity of God.* Written by John B. Metzger, published by Ariel Ministries in 2010, *www.Ariel.org,* (ISBN: 978-1-935174-04-2). Also available in e-Book Download.

4. *Messianic Christology.* Written by Dr. Arnold G. Fruchtenbaum and published by Ariel Ministries in 1998, www.Ariel.org.

5. *Jesus was a Jew.* Written by Dr. Arnold G. Fruchtenbaum and published by Ariel Ministries in 2010 (ISBN: 978-1-935174-02-8).

I know and understand the beliefs of Judaism, so I realize you may initially reject all this; but keep this book on hand, for there are two dynamic things that will happen in the near future (although the exact timing is unknown). First, a day will come when a large body of people from all nations of the earth will suddenly disappear, and secondly Israel will be attacked by Gog and Magog with no hope of survival (Ezekiel chapters 38 to 39). You will find this book and the others referenced very important as "Holocaust II" descends on the Jewish people. I am writing to you now because I love the Jewish people, Israel and the G-d of Israel.

Rev. John B. Metzger, M.A.

Appendix A:
How to Become
One with G-d

To Be Reconciled to G-d

It is my prayer that upon reading this book your heart has been stirred as you recognize Jesus of Nazareth as the incarnation of G-d; He is *HaShem*. It has been demonstrated throughout this book that He is G-d Almighty, *Yahweh*, the Messenger (Angel) of *Yahweh*, the Son of David who sits at the right hand of G-d, and the One for whom the Father will make His enemies His foot-stool (Psalm 110:1; Daniel 7:13-14). The vast majority of Jewish people have lost hope in the future reality of the literal coming of the *Moshiach*, and understandably so, for He came 2,000 years ago and was rejected because He did not come in the manner the rabbis and the people of that day expected Him to come.

Below are some verses referred to as the Jerusalem Road to lead you into embracing by faith the *Moshiach*, the Son of David, *Yeshua* as your Saviour from sin. I know you do not consider yourself a great sinner. But consider in your *Tanakh* the G-d of your fathers Abraham, Isaac and Jacob, who is absolutely Holy, Righteous, Just, and totally separated from sin. Open your Scripture and study His character. He originally gave to you—His covenant people, to you through your fathers—sacrifices and priests to mediate between them and Himself. Your fathers needed a mediator. What was the need for the sacrifices, and why did your fathers need a mediator to act on their behalf before

HaShem in His temple? It is because they were sinners and there was nothing they could do to merit favor before a sinless Holy Righteous G-d. Israel needed a substitute to take *HaShem's* wrath for their sins. That is what the sacrificial system was all about.

To sin against *HaShem* is simply man's disobedience against His Law and against *HaShem* Himself. You may call it the "evil inclination," but whatever you call it, it is simply missing the mark of G-d's holiness. In *HaShem's* eyes, little acts of sin are just as much sin as murder, for they are equally sin before a Holy G-d. Sinful things that you think or hide in your heart, even if you do not do them physically, are sins in *HaShem's* eyes. If you in your mind or heart have lusted after a woman, you have committed adultery in your heart before *HaShem.* You may not have broken the letter of the Law, but you have revealed the sinfulness of your heart and have broken the spirit of the Law. Ladies, if you covet something that is your neighbor's and want it to the point that you will obtain it at most any cost, *HaShem* judges that as sin. Notice that in neither of these examples was the act literally committed, yet *HaShem* views your heart from which comes wrong and evil. The words of *Yeshua the Jewish teacher* are found in the New Testament:

> *(18) But those things which proceed out of the mouth come forth from the heart; and they defile the man. (19) For out of the heart proceed evil thoughts, murders, adulteries, fornication, thefts, false witness, blasphemies* (Matthew 15:18-19).

Also Hebrews, the New Testament book that was written to Jewish believers in Messiah in the first century of the Common Era, reflects the penetration of the Word of *HaShem* into the innermost part of our being:

(12) For the word of God is quick, and powerful, and sharper than any two edged sword, piercing even to the dividing asunder of the soul and spirit, and of the joints and marrow, and is a discerner of the thoughts and intents of the heart. (13) Neither is there any creature that is not manifest in his sight: but all things are naked and open unto the eyes of him with whom we have to do. (Hebrews 4:12-13)

That verse is simply stating that the Scriptures are like a double edged sword and can pierce into the spiritual part of man (soul and spirit), as well as the physical part of man (joints and marrow). It can even discern the very thoughts you think and the motivation behind them before you ever do them.

Nearly 2000 years ago *HaShem* allowed Rome to destroy the Holy City and the Holy Temple, just as He allowed Babylon centuries before to destroy Jerusalem and Solomon's Temple. When *HaShem* destroyed Jerusalem the first time, He gave Israel prophets like Jeremiah, Ezekiel, and Daniel. He also gave them prophets like Haggai, Zephaniah, Zechariah, and Malachi after the return from Babylon. *HaShem* destroyed Jerusalem because of the sin of His covenant people, Israel. Notice there has not been, from Judaism's perspective, a prophet to Israel since Malachi who lived 2,400 years ago.

Now if the sacrificial system was *HaShem's* picture of His Holy demands and man's complete inability to keep His laws, why did HaShem remove the sacrificial system which was absolutely necessary, and why did He not replace it or even give a prophet with a Word from Himself? Or did He give a Prophet (Deuteronomy 18:15-18) in the person of His Son (Psalm 2:7-12; Proverbs 30:4), the Suffering Servant of

Isaiah 53, the Servant of the *L-RD*? After the crucifixion of *Yeshua*, two of his disciples on the Emmaus Road had problems understanding the shameful death of *Yeshua*. Due to the teaching they had received from the Pharisees, they looked for a military leader to liberate them from Rome. Their lack of understanding was their problem; they had a wrong Jewish expectation. *Yeshua* never denied His coming to restore Israel. He first had to come and suffer and die. In rabbinic Judaism today, how do you get rid of your sins biblically? Rabbinic Judaism has supplanted the Word of *HaShem* by saying that repentance, good deeds and charity are in place of blood atonement. They try to substantiate that but the context of Scripture militates against their argument.

Back in Genesis 3:15, before there were Jewish people, before Abraham and the Covenant, *HaShem* spoke to Adam and Eve and promised a spiritual deliverer who would restore that paradise lost. *HaShem* must first deal with the curse of sin that plagues all of mankind. The rabbis have falsely taught that repentance, good deeds and charity replace sacrifice as the atonement. However, in the entire *Tanakh*, *HaShem* has never changed the way of atonement; it has always been by blood sacrifice (Leviticus 17:11). Before Israel can be restored and the promise fulfilled to Abraham, *HaShem* must fulfill His promise that Adam and Eve heard from the L-rd to restore the creation and mankind back to their original place. That meant that the *seed of the woman* would first deliver mankind spiritually by removing the sin that separated them from *HaShem* before Israel could be restored by the very same *seed of the woman*.

According to *Bereshit Rabba* 23, a rabbinic Commentary on Genesis:

Eve had respect to the seed which is coming from another place. And who is this? This is Messiah the King.

So the Scriptures actually had prophesied that *Moshiach* would be rejected (Psalms 22; Isaiah 52:13-53:12) and would die a shameful death before His glorification. Some of you know of the rabbinic messiahs who will come, the first one called Messiah ben Joseph who will suffer and die. Then rabbinic Judaism teaches that another messiah will follow who will reign as Messiah ben David. Since both rabbinic Judaism and *HaShem* speak of two messiahs, perhaps it would be a good idea to listen to the Word of *HaShem* rather than rabbinic Judaism, which has endorsed 46 false messiahs over the centuries. Rabbinic Judaism has made authoritative teachings that directly contradict *HaShem*. Since your eternal destiny is at stake, whose word is more important, the rabbis', or the Word of *HaShem* Himself? That is a question you must ask yourself. Where does my spiritual authority come from: the rabbis or *HaShem*? *HaShem* loves you with an everlasting love, and you are inscribed on the palm of His hand (Isaiah 49:16; Jeremiah 31:3-10)!

> *The LORD did not set his love upon you, nor choose you, because ye were more in number than any people; for ye were the fewest of all people: But because the LORD loved you, and because he would keep the oath which he had sworn unto your fathers.* (Deuteronomy 7:7-8)

> *For thus says the LORD of hosts, "After glory He has sent me against the nations which plunder you, for he who touches YOU, touches the apple of His eye.* (Zechariah 2:12)

205

Search the Scriptures and ask the G-d of your fathers to show you what He has written in His Word. Search for yourself *HaShem*'s Word that Moses and the prophets recorded concerning His Son, your *Moshiach*, the Son of David, the King of Israel, your substitutionary sacrifice for your sin. Allow *HaShem* to remove that which is eclipsing your view of Him. Most of the Scripture verses quoted below come from the *Tanakh*, the Harkavy Version published by the Hebrew Publishing Company, unless otherwise noted.

The Jerusalem Road

1. There is none without sin

Psalm 14:3

> They are all gone aside, they are all together become filthy: there is none that doeth good, no, not one.

Psalm 51:7 [5]

> Behold, I was shapen in iniquity; and in sin did my mother conceive me.

Isaiah 53:6

> All we like sheep have gone astray; we have turned every one to his own way; and the LORD hath caused the iniquity of us all to fall upon him.

Jeremiah 17:9

> The heart is deceitful above all things, and desperately sick: who can know it?

Isaiah 59:1-2

> *Behold, the LORD's hand is not shortened, that it cannot save; neither his ear heavy, that it cannot hear: But your iniquities have separated between you and your God, and your sins have hid his face from you, that he will not hear.*

Ecclesiastes 7:20

> *For there is not a just man upon earth, that doeth good, and sinneth not.*

2. Good deeds cannot purify

Isaiah 64:6

> *But we are all as an unclean thing, and all our righteousness is as a filthy garment; and we all do fade as a leaf; and our iniquities, like the wind, have taken us away.*

Habakkuk 2:4

> *Behold, his soul is haughty, it is not upright in him: but the just shall live by his faith.*

Jeremiah 18:20

> *Shall evil be recompensed for good? For they have dug a pit for my soul. Remember that I stood before thee to speak good for them, and to turn away their wrath from them.*

3. G-d requires a blood sacrifice

Leviticus 17:11

> *For the life of the flesh is in the blood: and I have given it to you upon the altar to make an atonement for your souls: for it is the blood that makes an atonement for the soul.*

4. Apply the blood of the Messiah

Exodus 12:21-23

> *Then Moses called for all the elders of Israel, and said unto them, Draw out and take you a lamb according to your families and kill the Passover. And ye shall take a bunch of hyssop, and dip it in the blood that is in the basin and strike the lintel and the two side posts with the blood that is in the basin; and none of you shall go out at the door of his house until morning. For the LORD will pass through to smite the Egyptians; and when he seeth the blood upon the lintel, and on the two side posts, the LORD will Passover the door, and will not suffer the destroyer to come in unto your houses to smite you.*

Leviticus 16:15-19

> *Then shall he kill the goat of the sin-offering, that is for the people, and bring his blood within the veil, and do with that blood as he did with the blood of the bullock, and sprinkle it upon the mercy seat, and before the mercy seat: And he shall make an atonement for the holy place, because of the uncleanness of the children of Israel, and because of their transgressions in all their sins: and so shall he*

do for the tabernacle of the congregation, that remaineth among them in the midst of their uncleanness. And there shall be no man in the tabernacle of the congregation when he goeth in to make an atonement in the holy place, until he come out, and have made an atonement for himself, and for his household, and for all the congregation of Israel. And he shall go out unto the altar that is before the LORD, and make an atonement for it; and shall take of the blood of the bullock, and of the blood of the goat, and put it upon the horns of the altar round about. And he shall sprinkle of the blood upon it with his finger seven times, and cleanse it, and hallow it from the uncleanness of the children of Israel.

Daniel 9:26

And after threescore and two weeks shall Messiah be cut off, but not for himself: and the people of the prince that shall come shall destroy the city and the sanctuary; and the end thereof shall be with a flood, and unto the end of the war desolations are determined.

Hebrews 9:12

Neither by the blood of goats and calves, but by his own blood he entered in once into the holy place, having obtained eternal redemption for us.

5. Safety and refuge in G-d's Messiah

Psalm 2:12

> *Kiss the Son, lest he be angry, and ye perish from the way, when his wrath is kindled but a little. Blessed are all they that put their trust in him.* (KJV)

Psalm 51:15 [13]

> *Then will I teach transgressors thy ways; and sinners shall be converted unto thee.*

Other Passages

Words of *Yeshua* [Jesus]:

John 3:3 – *Except a man be born again, he cannot see the kingdom of God.*

John 3:14-18 – *[14] And as Moses lifted up the serpent in the wilderness* (Number 21:5-9) *even so must the son of man be lifted up: [15] That whosoever believeth in him should not perish, but have eternal life. [16] For God so loved the world, that he gave his only begotten Son, that whosoever believeth in him should not perish, but have everlasting life. [17] For God sent not his Son into the world to condemn the world; but that the world through him might be saved. [18] He that believeth on him is not condemned: but he that believeth not is condemned already, because he hath not believed in the name of the only begotten Son of God.*

John 3:36 – *He that believeth on the Son hath everlasting life: and he that believeth not the Son shall not see life; but the wrath of God abideth on him.*

John 5:39 – *Search the Scriptures; for in them you think you have eternal life: and they are they which testify of me.*

John 5:46 – *For had you believed Moses, you would have believed me: for he wrote of me.*

John 8:24 – *I said therefore unto you, that you shall die in your sins: for if you believe not that I am, you shall die in your sins.*

John 14:6 – *Jesus said unto him, I am the way, the truth, and the life: no man comes to the Father, but by me.*

Peter's words about Jesus before the Sanhedrin:

Acts 4:12 – *Neither is there salvation in any other: for there is none other name under heaven given among men, whereby we must be saved.*

Paul's words concerning the Gospel:

I Corinthians 15:3-4 – *[3] For I delivered unto you first of all that which I also received, how that Messiah died for our sins according to the scriptures; [4] And that he was buried, and that he rose again the third day according to the scriptures.*

(All New Testament quotes from the King James Version)

Responding to G-d

Taking G-d's Word as a guide, how can we be reconciled to G-d as He has required of us? Call on *Yeshua* your Messiah in faith, believing that He came to die for your sin, He was buried and He rose again the third day as He promised. Embrace Him as your personal Saviour and the very Spirit of G-d will come and indwell and seal you until the day of redemption. What a glorious day.

It is advisable for believers in Messiah *Yeshua* to get a copy of the Bible and begin to study *HaShem*'s Word. Reading the Gospels: Matthew, Mark, Luke and John, is extremely important. To continue to grow, finding a congregation that worships is also important, whether it is with fellow Messianic believers or a congregation of believers that teaches from the Bible and not man's opinions or philosophies.

You can receive further guidance from some very good study material from Ariel Ministries taught from a Jewish perspective by Jewish believers in Messiah *Yeshua*. My prayer is that Jewish people will no longer be Eclipsed from their G-d.

John B. Metzger

A Gentile sinner saved by the
Grace of *HaShem* in a Jewish Messiah.

Appendix B:
Jesus Versus the
Oral Law

Jesus attacked the rabbinic position of the Oral Law. It was in existence in Jesus' day as it is in our day. Outside of Jesus claiming to be G-d, this is one of the primary reasons why the Sanhedrin despised *Yeshua*. Look at his emphasis on the inner man, the heart. As in the Hebrew Scriptures, the word *heart* is always in the singular. There are no evil and good inclinations; look at Jesus' words as He takes the Pharisees to task about elevating the Oral Law over *HaShem's* Word. These verses come from the Gospel of Mark 7:3-16 in the New Testament:

> *³ For the Pharisees, and all the Jews, except they wash their hands oft, eat not, holding the **tradition of the elders**.* *⁴ And when they come from the market, except they wash, they eat not. And many other things there be, which they have received to hold, as the washing of cups, and pots, brazen vessels, and of tables.* *⁵ Then the Pharisees and scribes asked him, Why walk not thy disciples according to the tradition of the elders, but eat bread with unwashed hands?* *⁶ He answered and said unto them, Well hath Isaiah prophesied of you hypocrites, as it is written, This people honoureth me with their lips, but their heart is far from me.*

7 Howbeit in vain do they worship me, **teaching for doctrines the commandments of men.** *8 For* **laying aside the commandment of God, you hold the tradition of men,** *as the washing of pots and cups: and many other such like things ye do. 9 And he said unto them, Full well* **you reject the commandment of God, that ye may keep your own tradition.** *10 For Moses said, Honour thy father and thy mother; and, Whoso curses father or mother, let him die the death: 11 But ye say, If a man shall say to his father or mother, It is Corban, that is to say, a gift, by whatsoever thou might be profited by me; he shall be free. 12 And ye suffer him no more to do ought for his father or his mother; 13* **Making the word of God of none effect through your tradition,** *which ye have delivered: and many such like things do ye. 14 And when he had called all the people unto him, he said unto them, Hearken unto me every one of you, and understand: 15 There is nothing from without a man, that entering into him can defile him: but the things which come out of him, those are they that defile the man. 16 If any man have ears to hear, let him hear.*

Jesus said that they were circumventing the Law of G-d, to elevate their own law. This was a common message of Jesus as He spoke to the people directly about it in the Sermon on the Mount in Matthew 5-7 as He contrasts the righteousness of *HaShem* to the righteousness of the Pharisees.

Appendix C:
Jewish People Who
Looked for Themselves

*"You have turned for me my mourning into dancing;
You have loosed my sackcloth and girded me with
gladness, That my soul may sing praise to You and
not be silent. O LORD my God, I will give thanks to
You forever."*

Psalm 30:11-12

Lauren B, Atlanta, GA

I grew up in a suburb of Baltimore, Maryland, where I was raised in a Conservadox Jewish home (between Conservative and Orthodox). My parents both came from traditional Jewish backgrounds. However, to me, religion was empty, unrewarding and devoid of the reality of G-d's presence.

By the time I entered college I was an agnostic. Shortly after graduation, I had a promising career at Borden Incorporated. Yet I felt that something was missing. During this time, I decided to pursue wholesome hobbies including learning to play the piano and read music.

Inspired by the *Jeopardy* television game show, I decided to make reading the Bible one of my new hobbies. I figured it would help me be well-rounded. Originally number 20 on the list (last), reading the Bible soon became number one!

Not owning a Bible, I asked a co-worker named Betsy, a Gentile believer who had been praying for me, if I could borrow one. She loaned me a Parallel Bible. At this point, I prayed and asked G-d—if He existed—to reveal Himself to me. The One I didn't believe existed began to draw me through His Word.

For six months, I pored over three different versions of the Book of Genesis. In the midst of that time, I was presented with a book titled, *Jesus in Genesis*. I was surprised that I couldn't quickly disprove the book's contention.

Surely the Lord was drawing me and wooing me to Himself. During Passover, an article about the local Messianic Jewish Congregation was in the newspaper. I was intrigued yet very cautious. Somehow, He led me to that Congregation, where Jews and Gentiles worship *Yeshua* (Jesus) the Messiah together. They loved me and prayed regularly for me. I wrestled with the question, "Is Jesus indeed the promised Messiah of Israel?" Several months later (Hanukkah, 1990) I placed my faith in Jesus as my personal Messiah and Redeemer. My new-found faith grew as I continued to read the Word and attend services.

Over a period of years, I began to grasp that I was eternally secure. After intensive study on the subject of assurance, I was overjoyed to know for certain that I have everlasting life. Jesus said, "He who believes in Me has everlasting life" (John 6:47). I learned that the reason He could fulfill such a wonderful promise is because when He died on the cross, *"the Lord laid on Him the iniquity of us all"* (Isaiah 53:6). When I believed in Him for eternal life, I entered into an incredibly beautiful and eternal relationship with the Lord.

Steve S, Pottstown, PA

My journey toward a spiritual relationship with G-d started with my mom. She grew up in an orthodox Jewish family. At a very young age I remember mom speaking about her upbringing and the questions she struggled with. For example, mom shared how her dad would not carry his umbrella on the Sabbath but had mom carry it for him. This, along with other inconsistencies, caused her to question her faith. Perhaps the most influential part she had in my spiritual journey was her desire to learn more about the promise found in Deuteronomy 18:15 where Moses said, *"The Lord thy G-d will raise up unto thee a Prophet from the midst of thee, of thy brethren, like unto me; unto Him ye shall hearken."* After being exposed to the teachings of the New Testament I placed my faith and trust in Jesus Christ as my Messiah. He is the One Moses spoke about as He alone fulfilled all the promises spoken about Him in the Old Testament.

John P, Pittsburgh, PA

My parents had been through the Holocaust and were married in 1946. I was born in [West] Germany the following year. One year later, my family traveled to Israel where we resided for the next six years. It was there that my mother led me to the Lord at the age of 5. I was then baptized two years later.

Not too long after that, I traveled to England and then returned to Germany after two years. It was there that my brother was born, a hydrocephalic. For his survival's sake, our family immigrated to the U.S. in 1962 so he would get the proper surgical care needed. We thank G-d that after seven major surgeries my brother Peter is alive today and leads a normal life.

During this time I had enrolled at the Washington Bible College (WBC) to prepare for whatever ministry the Lord would have for me. I majored in missions. Towards the latter years there I met the lady who would soon become my wife (we have now been married for 41 years). There also the Lord burdened my heart to study the Old Testament, which was also confirmed by a visiting chapel speaker: Dr. John Whitcomb from Grace Theological Seminary (GTS). Immediately after graduation from WBC, I enrolled at GTS, where I studied for the next 5 years.

Soon after graduation, the Lord placed me in the pastorate—as a matter of fact, five pastorates over the next 30 years! During this time, the Lord gave us two wonderful daughters, I taught some courses at a Bible college in Baltimore, a number of people came to know the Lord and grew in Him, I completed my class work at Dallas Theological Seminary in the D. Min. program, began writing articles in a few Pennsylvania weeklies and taught courses at Penn State for eight years as an adjunct at two campuses.

I "retired" approximately seven years ago from being a "full-time" pastorate, but not from serving the Lord. I am currently involved in several ministries and would like to utilize the gifts of teaching, writing and preaching for His glory as He opens doors of opportunity.

Itai R, New York City

Born and raised in Israel as a secular Jew, my family migrated to the US when I was 16. At 29, a friend invited me to a Thanksgiving service at a local church. There I first started reading about the life and teachings of Jesus from the Bible in the pew. My friend later also gave me a copy of the New Testament to have as my own. Four truths have struck a strong chord in my mind in the early days, and made a lot of sense to someone coming from a Jewish background:

1) Kosher to G-d is not defined by the food that we eat, but by the words that proceed from our mouth (Matthew 15:11).

2) Sabbath was designed for rest, and not for a legalistic list of do-not-do's (Mark 2:27-28).

3) G-d's commandments and desires for men, have been turned into doctrines and traditions of men that G-d is not pleased with (Mark 7:7-9).

4) What makes one a true Jew is the circumcision of the heart and not that of the flesh (Romans 2:28-29).

Later that year I studied how the concept of the Trinity exists right within the Genesis account of creation: G-d, the Word, and the hovering Spirit. I also saw how Jesus was the guiltless Lamb of G-d brought to the slaughter for man's sin, as was also described in Isaiah 53, and the Egypt Passover account. Despite all that understanding of G-d's truth, and attending regular church services, I only knew "about" Jesus.

One year later I became truly born again when conviction struck and I realized that "Jesus IS G-d", why you ask ? Because he is the only man to be born sinless, to die for the cause of covering man's sin, and to live wholly as a teaching tool manifesting man's salvation plan right inside his "actual" life and death and not simply only by his teachings. Yes, Jesus IS G-d, he is the only G-d, and only he can take away sin. He now became my G-d, I believed "in"

Jesus and I put my faith in the death of Christ the Saviour. The *LORD* indeed is my shepherd, I shall not lack.

Herschel L, Philadelphia, PA

Having been born to Jewish parents in Vienna, Austria, and a holocaust survivor, our family emigrated to the United States in 1939. We became assimilated in a predominately Gentilized world with very little connection with the Jewish community. In high school I was drawn to a person who brought his Bible to school every day and always placed it on the top of his other books. Over the course of a year we became friends, had many conversations about G-d, and he urged me to begin reading the Bible. I did. The passages that spoke to my heart were Isaiah 53, Jeremiah 29:13, the Gospel of John and Revelation 3:20.

Luda F, New York City

I became a believer after leaving the Soviet Union, and meeting some Christian nurses in New Zealand. I started to read the Bible and prayed a prayer my Christian friends suggested, asking Jesus, "If you are the Messiah, come into my life."

Everything became new for me after that, and I knew I was changed. I did not know much about the Bible, so I was really amazed to read the prophecies of Isaiah, which so clearly described Jesus. I remember especially reading Isaiah 9 and realizing it could only be talking about Jesus, and only if he is G-d, because it talks about someone named "Wonderful Counselor, Mighty G-d, Everlasting Father" yet it describes a person that is born as a human baby: *"for a child is born to us and a son is given to us, and the government will be upon his shoulder."* This verse and others, as I read more of the Bible, convinced me more than ever that Jesus was truly the Messiah and G-d.

Robert M, Los Angeles, CA

I came to trust in *Yeshua* as my personal Messiah and Savior from sin because I was looking for the truth. Although Jewish, I was unfamiliar with the Bible. However, when confronted with the message of the Bible I could see instantly that it was the truth. Why? Because it dealt with the real world of fallible human beings honestly. No whitewashing! I expected to read about perfect people, instead I discovered it dealt with people just like me. If it dealt with the world and with people accurately, then it must deal with G-d truthfully as well. Therefore, forgiveness of sins and the gift of eternal life through *Yeshua* was genuine, if I wanted to receive it. I did receive *Yeshua* and the truth of the Bible has become ever more precious and obvious to me as my 45 years as a Believer have passed one by one. *Yeshua* is the Way, the Truth and the Life.

Samuel N, Charlotte, NC

I was raised in a traditional Jewish home in Queens, NY, and I was therefore bar mitzvah according to Orthodox Jewish tradition. But I went from being religious to being quite rebellious, and became an atheist, thinking all religion was false. After I returned from serving our country in Viet Nam, I was working in a saloon in Eureka, CA. It was there someone first shared Messiah with me. Though I laughed and mocked that person, unbeknownst to me, a seed was planted in my heart.

Months later in San Francisco, I was invited to a Bible study. I went to it just to mock the people there. They showed me Isaiah 53. At that time, though, I told these believers that it made no sense to me, but in fact Isaiah 53 made me very curious … and quite concerned that it might just be true. Several months after that, and after attempting to disprove it, I came to believe G-d's Word and trusted *Yeshua* as my Lord and Savior.

David G, Indianapolis, IN

Both of my parents were born into Jewish homes, but after they met and married, they ended up moving to Japan where they were influenced by Zen Buddhism. Consequently, although I knew that I was Jewish when I was growing up, the only time I was able to really participate in services or the High Holidays was when we were invited to my relatives' house. I very much enjoyed those times.

However, when I was 14, we were back in Japan when my mother passed away. After my father finished his contract, we returned to the U.S. when I was 16, and my father announced that we were going back to the synagogue. The one we attended was a conservative synagogue in Lafayette, Indiana, and I enjoyed the weekly services and all the holidays.

In college, I stopped going to synagogue on a regular basis, but still tried to make Passover and the High Holidays. Then, in my senior year, I met a Jewish girl and after dating through that year and through my two years of graduate school, we decided to get married. It looked like my life as a Jew was set.

However, G-d had other plans. Those plans included our forgoing our marriage plans, my meeting a nice Gentile girl three weeks before I was leaving for Japan to take a 2-year teaching contract, my meeting her parents the evening before I left, the two of us writing almost every day, her visiting me during the winter and the two of us deciding to get married. I know that seems strange, but that is what happened.

After we married in 1983, for the first 10 years of our marriage, I went to synagogue on occasion and she went to church. Sometimes I went to the church service, but it made me very nervous, especially if there was Communion. Then, after those 10 years, the Lord must have decided it was time. My wife received a post card from a Messianic Congregation that stated that the most Jewish thing you could do as a Jew was to believe in *Yeshua*, the Jewish Messiah. Well, after my getting over being very upset, the Rabbi and his wife ended up coming over, and after that meeting, I started to attend the Messianic congregation located in the Detroit area. After 6 months, I knew the New Testament was true, and after about one more year of study and wrestling with different aspects, I became a believer in *Yeshua*, in May 1994.

Today, Praise G-d, I am still attending that congregation with my wife and our youngest daughter. Our eldest daughter graduated Moody Bible Institute, in the Jewish Studies program, married a nice Jewish boy and they both work for Ariel Ministries as he continues his education at Dallas Theological Seminary. I am so grateful to the Lord for helping me break the generational bond of unbelief that existed in my family through discovering our wonderful Messiah *Yeshua*.

Appendix D:
Historical Background
for Gentile Christian
Readers

Historical Enmity

Context: This book is written to Jewish people, and that is the context of this book. I am presenting a message of love and concern, dealing with difficult questions that require a search for truth. What does G-d's Word say about the future for the Jewish people? The message seems shrouded in mystery and misunderstanding, both to Jewish people and Christians as well.

Approach: It is not my intention to offend any Christian or any Jewish person, but understanding truth must always be given first priority. As a Christian minister I am responsible to rightly divide the Word of truth, even if that truth makes us uncomfortable. Without an understanding of the history between the Church and the Jewish people, most Christians will be offended by my negative comments about the Church.

The truth is that many chapters of the historic Church have been negative towards Jewish people. These negative chapters are mostly unknown to Gentile (non-Jewish) Christians, and most Church history books are mute on the subject; but Jewish people are very aware of the history of persecution that resulted from unbiblical teachings and philosophies that have influenced the Church.

Warning: What I have presented in this book may be offensive to you and may diminish your interest in reading this book. To you it will seem harsh and unjustified, but let me assure you that in their relations to the Jewish people, the historic Church has brought great shame to the name of Christ (Messiah).

Preparation: So Christian readers, if necessary, please read up on Church history in relation to Jewish people. I have included a list of excellent references on this topic. By understanding the Jewish perspective, you will more likely find the pages in this book instructive and challenging, rather than confusing or offensive.

John B. Metzger

Recommended Readings
on Church History and the Jewish People

Baleston, Mottel. *The Holocaust: History and Theology* (San Antonio, TX: Ariel Ministries, 2007), DVD.

Brown, Michael. *Our Hands are stained with Blood* (Shippensburg, PA: Destiny Image Publications, 1992), ISBN: 1-56043-068-0.

Dimont, Max. *Jews, God and History* (New York: Mentor Book, 1994), ISBN: 0-451-62866-7.

Feinberg, Charles L. *Israel: At the Center of History & Revelation* (Portland, OR: Multnomah Press, 1980), 130-138. ISBN: 0-930014-38-3.

Heinrich, William H. *In the Shame of Jesus* (Morgantown, PA: Masthof Press, 2008), ISBN: 978-1-60126-176-2.

Horner, Barry E. *Future Israel: Why Christian Anti-Judaism Must Be Challenged* (Nashville, TN: B&H Academic, 2007), ISBN: 978-0-8054-4627-2.

Melnick, Oliver. *They Have Conspired Against You, Responding to the New Anti-Semitism* (Huntington Beach, CA: Purple Raiment label of JHousePublishing, 2007), ISBN: 0-9765252-1-6.

Rydelnik, Michael. *They called Me Christ Killer* (Grand Rapids, MI: Discovery Series, Radio Bible Class, 2005).

Telchin, Stan, *Betrayed* (Grand Rapids, MI: Chosen Books, 2007), ISBN: 0-8007942-30.